Ace the Sale!
a Practical Methodology for Selling B2B Enterprise Software, Hardware or Services

Don't hack your way around the sales cycle!

by Nick Gomersall

Published in 2011 by Bennion Kearny Limited.

ISBN: 978-0-9559114-3-9

Published by Bennion Kearny Limited
6 Victory House
64 Trafalgar Road
Birmingham
B13 8BU

www.BennionKearny.com

Cover image: ©iStockphoto.com/jostaphot

Acknowledgements

Thank you to all the people that reviewed this book and the input that I was given, especially in remembering some of the funny stories that you will find throughout Ace the Sale.

In total, this book enjoyed the evaluation, wisdom and advice of almost a dozen people, and for those who I cannot name directly – many thanks for your excellent help.

For those whom I can name, I would like to thank in particular Matt Crotty "Chairman of InsightSoftware.com" who I have worked for in a number of ventures for almost 14 years in total. Matt always gave me the freedom to express myself and allowed me to make mistakes in my early selling career which taught me many a valuable lesson. I would also like to express my gratitude to Nick Rawls who I worked with in the days of JD Edwards for his input, and my daughter Hannah Stone who is now embarking on her own quest to be an Ace sales rep.

In turn, many thanks to Chris Golis the author of *Empathy Selling* which was instrumental in helping drive success at JD Edwards and The GL Company, and Sam Reese the CEO of Miller Heiman who has kindly allowed the reproduction of some of their sales methodology in this book.

Thank you Mr "C" who is still selling today and was worried should one of his prospects ever buy this book and see that he had been credited (and maybe lose a deal). An exceptional sales guy who I shared many a sales campaign with (and a lot of laughs). "Thanks (C)hris!"

Last but not least to my publisher Bennion Kearny who, without their help, this book would never have been written.

About the author

The short version

After spending five years trying to qualify as a chartered accountant I changed career and joined the fledging computer industry. Exams were no boundary for promotion here but soon I found out that my personality was best suited to sales. Learning the hard way, by making mistakes, enabled me to land the best job of my life. I joined JD Edwards as the first European employee. I became sales director for Northern Europe and ten years of selling experience in this company set me up for life. When I left, the JD Edwards experience enabled me to turn a struggling consultancy company into one of The Times' fastest growing Tech 100 companies in the UK.

The longer version

I started life as an articled clerk in a firm of City Accountants. After 5 years and having failed the final exam, I decided to change career and joined Star Computers as a client adviser, installing software and training people on bookkeeping systems for the accounting profession.

Dealing with unhappy customers in the early eighties was like being on the switchboard of the Samaritans as these new mini computer systems had many issues and all you could do was console the customer over the phone. Then one day I went over to the sales department to inform a sales representative about a problem with their account.

It was 4 o'clock in the afternoon, and I was surprised that no one was in the office. "They are down the pub," someone told me, and 10 minutes later the sales team returned to the office, celebrating a great first quarter. This looked like an interesting career and there was no way back. *Sales* was where my future lay.

In 1982 I joined an IBM software house called Insight Database Systems (IDS) as the customer support manager which was a really tough job and one that has been described in the 19th hole (revisited).

Luckily for me, because of my accountancy knowledge I was able to do the complex presales work for the sales team. Because I was making money for them I was totally bullet proof - protected by the international sales manager and his team. It did not take me too long to move into a full time role in presales where I was a hero (self-described) in all the demos but did not pick up the big commission checks that were flying around.

So when an opportunity arose for launching a brand new Business Intelligence (BI) system for the chairman of IDS I took it, single-handedly generating over $1m of new BI sales in a product called Advanced Management Information System (AMIS), for the IBM AS/400 back in 1980s. I did my own cold calling, sales presentations, management of the sales cycle and closing. It was a great challenge. Coming from accounting and presales backgrounds did help and the 5 years of accounting experience proved to be of great value.

One of the more interesting closes was when I built a manpower manning model with AMIS for a high street retailer on a one month trial. When I told them the software was being deleted off their server they signed the order there and then. "Nick we need all this information for a board meeting next month," said the CIO, quickly signing the order.

Gomersall: AMIS is quick and easy. Picture reproduced from System 3X TODAY, June 1987. Management science meets the System 38.

I ran the AMIS division at IDS where I managed a team of presales and sales people before the company was sold to Hoskyns, now Cap Gemini.

From IDS, I ran the European and Asia Pacific region for Data 3 - a MRP 11 software house (Now called ERP). The whole sales channel was run through partners and managing these guys was a challenge. Partner channels normally don't have great sales teams so implementing a sales process is vital if you are to have any chance of accurately forecasting business.

An example of just how bad a channel can be was when the Spanish agent needed a big discount for a Spanish Charity.

"How much do you need, Miguel?" I asked.

"100%," was the reply. "They will be a great reference and it would be good for getting into Spain."

After a few weeks explaining to the head of sales in the US that this might be a good idea, I finally got approval to give the software away. I had a conference call with Miguel and asked how the Spanish Charity was doing? "Nick, I have bad news. We have lost the deal," was his reply. I was not looking forward to the next forecast meeting with my US boss to explain to him why we lost a deal to another vendor giving our software away! Maybe they paid the charity to take their software!

Data3 was sold to ASK (Now Computer Associates) and in 1990 I joined JD Edwards as their first European employee. JD Edwards was, and still is, one of the leading ERP providers. I had a number of roles at JD Edwards in my ten years at the company and won many performance club awards.

One of my roles was to manage a team of 14 sales reps and 7 pre sales people in the UK with a sales target of over $50m. That year *every* sales rep hit their number. I was featured in Salesforce magazine about how the team achieved this performance, and how we used to allocate leads to the sales team on a needs basis and who would get on best with the prospect. Far too many good sales reps don't perform at the top of their game because their territory is bad whereas a bad sales rep can make their number because they have a better patch.

Nick featured in Salesforce magazine in 1997

Afterwards, I managed the green team business unit which was responsible for launching the new open systems OneWorld Product (now E1) again smashing the sales number, with everyone in the team making club. I was also responsible for the sales and marketing for the SUMA (Scandinavia, UK, Middle East and Africa) region as well as being marketing Director for Europe. JD Edwards was a great place to be - a company that had compound growth of 60% each year growing from a turnover of $40m worldwide when I joined to over $934m when it went public in September 1997.

Success was down to building a great team with high Emotional Intelligence and a great sales process. All sales reps qualified hard and achieved a close rate of 80% on what they bid on. This was highlighted when PeopleSoft took over JD Edwards in 2003 where in the UK they employed twice as many sales and presales people than JD Edwards in order to hit the same target number.

After 10 years at JD Edwards I rejoined the chairman of IDS to see if we could turn around a loss making consultancy company with a turnover of £1.2m, and losses of over £2m. I was given a final £250k of capital and six months to see if it was worth saving.

What to do? We changed the company from a service orientated consultancy organization to a product focused organization, initially on the JD Edwards market. Turnover rose to over £8m in product sales, and there were consistent profits and positive cash flow. This company was initially called The GL Company and has since been renamed to Insight Software (note the similar name to the Chairman's first software house) and is a dominant player in the JD Edwards and Oracle E Business Suite market.

In 2007 I left The GL Company as it entered The Times' top tech 100 fastest growing private UK companies.

Successes were achieved without employing a single professional salesperson; we simply used all the techniques you will be reading about in this book. Techniques that turned presales people and consultants into one of the best sales forces in the market.

Please visit
www.AcetheSale.co.uk
for book information, links,
contacting the author, and more.

Table of contents

Preface

I will always remember the best piece of professional advice that I ever received.

There are only two things that you need to succeed in corporate life:

1. *Always make sure that your boss is happy.*
2. *Learn to play golf.*

It's not always easy keeping your boss happy but as a golfer from an early age I had the second part covered. When I was managing sales reps and dealing with prospects, not only would a round of golf help close a deal or smooth over a problem – I learned that what you face on the golf course is exactly what you find in a sales cycle.

As they say: *you can't win a golf tournament on the first day, but you sure can lose it*. If you don't get the sales process right - from the start - then the chances of winning are slim. Welcome to the Ace the Sale, a methodology for selling B2B software, hardware or services.

Ace the Sale has been based around my experience in selling software, services and (in my early career) hardware. As hardware became a commodity my focus changed to just software and services. The principles that are found in this book though are relevant to any type of Business-to-Business sale where multiple buyers are involved in making a purchasing decision. Although the stories and anecdotes relate mainly to software deals, the principles behind them hold true for the other types of sale highlighted.

Who this book is for

This book is for you if you are engaged in the selling or sales management of major capital projects, software, or services that have multiple people involved in the buying process.

- This book is primarily aimed at *sales reps*, and offers practical real-world advice and strategies that close more business.
- There is also lots of information in this book for when sales reps move up the corporate ladder and become *sales managers*. Existing sales managers should also find valuable information in the methodology.

Ace the Sale is about turning ordinary sales reps into tournament pros, and good sales reps into world beaters who can consistently win new business.

Co-existing with existing sales methodologies

This book is designed to be a fast track guide that will complement some existing sales methodologies, or even become one of its own. The information is structured around a 'round of golf' – a hole by hole approach to the sales cycle and sales success.

Each hole represents a step towards a 'close' that I believe to be critical to sales success. In turn, I have tried to include lots of stories and anecdotes ('On the tee' sections) to show the principles in action which hopefully makes reading this book more fun and very different from normal archetypal sales books.

There are times where I might suggest marketing strategies or tactics that need to be implemented by management which will be out of your control as a sales rep. These ideas should be brought up and discussed at sales meetings to instigate change if need be. I will point these out along the way and you never know, these suggestions just might help push along your promotion.

What we will cover

Let's go through what each hole will cover. Don't let my golf analysis put you off this book - if you are a non-golfer or hate the game, just treat these holes as 18 steps towards a successful close.

The 19th Hole - **The Clubhouse**
Normally 'played' at the end of the round but we'll tackle it first. On this hole you will see that there are many times when you should head straight off the course, maybe even in the middle of a round!

The 1st Hole (par 5) - **The Right Equipment**
Without the right equipment you won't shoot low. We will be discussing what a good

sales process can do for you together with the value of embedding information into a Customer Relationship Management (CRM) system.

The 2nd Hole (par 5) - **Emotional Intelligence**
Emotional Intelligence (EQ). Are you born with it or can it be learned? Great sales people have EQ; but can you learn to have empathy and communication skills if you aren't a natural?

The 3rd Hole (Par 4) - **Competition**
Knowing your own strengths and weaknesses is essential; but are you studying the competition hard enough as well?

The 4th Hole (Par 4) - **What's your Sandwich? Why Good Marketing Matters**
Marketing will generate the leads that supply the sales team; but who is in control, and what can be done to ensure the sales team has the fuel to drive business?

The 5th Hole (Par 4) - **The First Meeting is Critical**
Meeting your prospect for the first time can tee you up for success. Setting the right level of expectation will ensure no surprises later in the sales cycle.

The 6th Hole (Par 4) - **The First Presentation**
Meeting all the decision makers for the first time will enable you to find out who the movers and shakers are. Find out how to spot the informal hierarchy of your potential customer and why cultivating 'the weakest link' will give you strength in the sales cycle.

The 7th Hole (Par 5) - **How are we Doing?**
How are we doing? Here we will look at a process that enables us to take a critical look at just how well we are progressing on an account, and what needs to be done to ensure success.

The 8th Hole (Par 3) - **Commit to the deal, Multi-Level Selling**
Doing anything half-heartedly will not bring results. Understand why working on fewer deals will generate better returns.

The 9th Hole (Par 3) - **Last One through the Door**
Continuous communication with your prospect is essential and you need to make sure that you always have the last word. This hole will lay the foundations for you to ensure that you always have a valid purchasing reason to call your prospects.

The 10th Hole (Par 5) - **Do you need Birdies or Pars?**
The game does not start until the last nine holes on the last day. Have you got your strategy right, do you need to walk, or can you get *part* of the deal? If you are winning you need to close as soon as you can, if you are losing you need to delay the sales cycle.

The 11th Hole (Par 4) - **Complex Pricing and Clauses you don't need**
Complex pricing and clauses in the contract you don't need will ensure you leave little money on the table and enjoy a smoother negotiation.

The 12th Hole (Par 4) - **Internal Selling: why is it so important?**
Selling internally is just as important as external sales if you want presales and management support.

The 13th Hole (Par 4) - **The Final Presentation**
The final presentation is the last time you will see all the buyers together in one room. Don't miss out on this opportunity to show them that your solution will solve their individual issues.

The 14th Hole (Par 3) - **The Reference Visit**
The reference visit will sort out the men from the boys. Have you got a user base that will be willing to help? Have you spent enough time with your customer?

The 15th Hole (Par 3) - **The Board Presentation**
The board presentation is your last opportunity to influence the key decision makers. Presenting in a relaxed manner will show confidence but you need to plan and prepare fully beforehand to pull this off.

The 16th Hole (Par 3) - **Decision Time**
Decision time is like waiting for your exam results, there is nothing you can do. If you lose - do you have a strategy?

The 17th Hole (Par 5) - **The Negotiation**
Negotiation is the most fun part of the sales cycle but some prospects take it more seriously than others.

The 18th Hole (Par 4) - **Contract Signature**
Getting the contract signed and the cash in your hand is sometimes harder than you might think. Don't delay. Go down and wait in reception if you have to, and collect the signed contract.

The 19th Hole (again) - **The Clubhouse Revisited**
Revisiting the 19th after a long and successful sale campaign is essential and here is the place when you can share your funny sales stories and celebrate your wins.

Appendix A - **The Empathy Selling Questionnaire**

Appendix B - **Sample Large Account Strategy and Sales Splits**

Terminology

If you already know your golf terms, feel free to play through this section. For those of you who don't play golf you'll notice how this book uses some golf terminology here and there. It's not critical if you don't know the terms fully, as principles will be laid out anyway. But it is worth taking a moment here to explain some basic expressions. Here is a super quick primer.

A golf course has eighteen holes and each hole has an optimum number of strokes (shots) that a player must take in order to get the ball in the hole.

A par three, for example, is a short hole and requires three strokes. This may be made up of one shot to the green and two putts. If you took three strokes to get the ball in the hole, it is called a par. If you do this in one shot under par (i.e. 2 strokes) it is called a *birdie* and two shots under par is called an *eagle*. If however you take one more shot than the par, then this is called a bogey, two over the par is a double bogey, and so on.

You want to get the ball around the course in the fewest number of strokes, and to do that you use different golf clubs. Drivers which send the ball a long way and which are used off the tee (the tee is where you start on every hole) to putters which you use on the greens (where the holes are).

There are normally par threes, fours and fives that make up the eighteen holes. So a typical golf course might have six par threes, four par fives and eight par fours. Each hole, once you are on the green, should only take two putts.

Okay, so that's everything we need to cover right now. Let's get to the 19th. Yes, the 19th!

The 19th hole

The Clubhouse

The Nineteenth Hole. Also known as the clubhouse, pub, coffeehouse, restaurant, or bar. It's the place you go to celebrate or drown sorrows, unwind and socialize. You might think it strange to start this book off with the 19th hole, but there are many times in a sales cycle when you need to head straight here. Let me explain.

Bad vibes

Back in the days of JD Edwards, my team and I were selling to a major UK PLC. We had made it down to the last two suppliers (from a shortlist of five), and planned a live demonstration at the customer's site. Gordon, my sales representative, was going to visit the customer the day before our big pitch, to load our software onto their system in preparation of a live demo utilising their data. I was concerned that he was leaving it a bit tight but he told me not to worry; everything would be okay, and it would soon be up and running.

During the installation, he picked up seriously bad vibes from the IT manager who clearly wanted the other supplier. *No worries* we thought. We had it all to do but we were confident that we could get enough support from the user community once they saw the demonstration, and turn the account around.

On the day of the demonstration the presales team, who were doing the presentation, arrived early but when I met Gordon he was looking very anxious.

"Nick," he said. "I have not been able to load the software. I just don't know what has gone wrong."

As he said this, I could see the IT manager coming my way and noticed a certain pleasure in our misfortune wrapped all across his face!

We were in a hopeless situation. With no software to show off, it looked as if the IT manager had won, and we would be forced to abandon the presentation. However, I was not going to give him the satisfaction of us just walking away - so come hell or high water - we were going to give a presentation of the software. We handed out the user manuals and began to go through them chapter by chapter. We lasted five minutes before the CIO stopped us, and said:

"Nick, this really is not working, is it?"

I agreed, apologised, and we left. As we went to the car park, Gordon was expecting a roasting, and the presales team were all looking fearful at what was going to happen next. We had clearly been sabotaged by the IT manager, and if he had made an effort to cooperate - the software would have loaded.

Rather than going back to the office to sulk all afternoon I decided to take the team out for a long lunch. Off we went to the 19th, where we had a great afternoon. We ate, we drank, and we talked. Gordon resolved to never make the mistake of loading software *the day before* any demonstration, the presales team had the afternoon off, and we all bonded and became determined never to lose a deal to our rival supplier again. It was moments like this when working at JD Edwards proved so much fun (as well as hard work). It was no surprise that the average length of service at this great company was 10 years plus.

So we walked off the course on the 10th, missed the cut, but we learned our lessons and were better prepared for out next game. We enjoyed a 90% success rate going forward against the competitor who had won this battle but not the war.

No clause, no deal

1992 was a great year for the SUMA team (Scandinavia, United Kingdom, Middle East and Africa) at JD Edwards and we had done our numbers two months before the year end. There was no doubt that we would win area of the year, and we were 300% ahead of quota in the Scandinavia area alone with one deal left to close before our year end.

One of the sales reps and I were just doing the final negotiations with a Swedish pharmaceutical company when Hendrick, the purchasing manager, wanted a *liability clause* in the contract in case anything went wrong. Hendrick had agreed all the points in the contract except this one.

"I want a clause in the contract that you accept liability, if something goes wrong," he said.

"We can't have an open ended liability clause in the contract," I answered. "We need to know exactly what it is that you are concerned could go wrong. Plus we need to set a limit on this. What value were you thinking?"

"Oh," replied Hendrick. He moved straight to the value of the liability: "around $20k should do it."

We were a week away from our year end, so I said to Hendrick: "tell you what, let's call this $20k an 'additional discount' and we can then sign the contract without this clause."

To our surprise Hendrick said: “No, I want this in the contract.”

“So you want a clause that stipulates if anything goes wrong, but we don’t know what, then you get $20k?”

“Yes.”

Now if you have ever worked with a US company you will know that getting a clause through without quantifying ‘what it is that might go wrong’ is never going to fly. We both knew this deal was not going to be booked unless we could get Hendrick to move and take the discount.

We persisted and tried to point out that getting the $20k now is better than if he had a clause in the contract. After all, chances were that everything would go well and he would not get the $20k later on.

He went off to discuss this with his financial director and then came back insisting that they needed this clause and that our competitor was willing to accept this. There was no way that HQ was going to book this deal with a contingent liability in the contract tied to Hendrick’s interpretation of something going wrong. We were getting nowhere and I turned around to my sales rep and said: “Are you thirsty?”

“Yes,” came the reply.

We had both come to the same conclusion. We were not going to be able to do business with these guys over a contractual issue, so we might as well be spending our time better, elsewhere. We got up, shook Hendrick’s hand and left him there in the boardroom.

The 19th hole (that day) was a wonderful piano bar in Stockholm where we had some of the best gin and tonics we have ever had. I rang the office and one of the sales guys picked up. “Listen to this Old Boy,” I said. I held up the handset as the sound of the piano drifted into the receiver and was relayed back to the guys in the UK. “I just wanted to kick off the celebrations early, guys. Well done on a great year! We have smashed our numbers.”

So the celebrations began, and the UK mob went off to their 19th knowing that you need to savour the positive moments, as next year’s targets were going to be higher and we would all start from zero in a week’s time. I turned to my sales guy: “I wonder if Hendrick is still waiting in the boardroom?” I said.

“Who cares,” was the reply. “Cheers!”

Although this example might look a bit blasé, walking from deals that could represent trouble is important. Problem customers take up much more management time when they start the installation especially if you are dealing with a client that thinks a contract is more important than having a relationship with your company.

Walking away also flushes out other issues which you will see further down the course. As a sales rep you will need to have the support of management to do a walk away, and I have one more story for you.

On the tee

We had lost a deal to one of our competitors due to them lying over the capabilities of their software. Six months later the prospect was back saying that the software they had bought did not do what they wanted (what a surprise) and they would like to come back and take another look at our solution. Peter the sales rep and John the presales person started to take the project manager through the software but he was so aggressive, challenging everything John was saying and being extremely obnoxious.

Peter stopped the demo. “You will have to leave,” he said.

“What do you mean?” replied the confused prospect. He could not believe what he had just heard.

“We don’t want you as a customer, you will have to go,” explained Peter, before escorting him off the premises.

At the time I was not responsible for this sale so Peter went straight into the CEO’s office and told him what had happened and said you will be getting a phone call in a few moments and asked him for his support. The phone call came and he duly supported Peter with a short to-the-point conversation to the prospect.

The CEO, Peter and John then went off to the 19th for an early lunch and Peter’s decision had saved the company time, money and a customer that would have been a nightmare to manage.

Summary

Managing a sales and presales team can be done in many ways. My style was to recruit great people and be as supportive as possible. In turn, when things go wrong and people think that angry reprimands are coming - *doing the opposite can have a better, longer lasting effect.*

Gordon who loaded the software the day before the demo ended up being the UK managing director and a VP for JD Edwards and PeopleSoft. He has since gone on to other senior management roles and I am sure that what we did that lunchtime had a far more motivating effect than if I had gone mad at him. We learn from our failures; they rarely need to be underscored with shouting or retribution.

The competitor that picked up the Swedish contract went into administration a few years later and the pharmaceutical company had a great contract but no software.

By throwing out the aggressive prospect Peter saved the company from a customer that would have drained our resources, and where we would have probably had ended up in litigation anyway.

We will be making many visits to the 19th hole throughout this book but now we must move onto the first tee where we will be looking at our golfing equipment because without the best equipment then there can be no victory. Let’s play!

The **1** st hole

The Right Equipment

It is really important to get off to a good start from the first tee. If you have got the wrong equipment then your chances of closing any sale are going to be made all the harder. For the majority of people you will have no choice in what you use - especially if you are working for a Fortune 500 company. You may need to improvise with a hybrid club or two as you will see later on this hole.

Driver or iron off the first

As I sit down and write the first hole I realise that I might upset a few people; the management that implemented your current Customer Relationship Management (CRM) system, for example. I am going to advocate times when you should use Excel and Outlook to overcome CRM issues, and this might not be popular reading. Criticisms of heavy duty CRM systems that benefit the company's reporting - rather than the sales rep's ability to generate business - just might not go down too well.

So maybe I should take an iron off the tee here and try to please everyone? Try not to be too controversial? Well, I am a bit like Phil Mickelson - it's just not my style and I owe it to the sales rep struggling with a poor CRM system to point these issues out. You never know, this book just might help you to change the way your CRM system is set up in your company.

This is what I believe:

> *No* sales? *No numbers to count! Sales come first.*
> If sales don't come first, the company won't survive. Therefore, the CRM system has to be sales led.

So I am hitting driver and going for birdies, let's hope I can pull it off!

What this hole will cover

Okay – you are now on the course, and you have a sales lead. But before you can start any sales cycle you need to have two things:

- A sales methodology.
- A software system (CRM) to track and monitor the progress of the sale.

A sales methodology will ensure that everyone in the company is speaking the same language and that you are following a proven process. A good CRM system will capture all the steps that are in the methodology, be easy to use, and help the sales reps run the sales campaigns.

I am not a great believer in filling out endless sales forms as they are seldom completed fully. But ticking boxes in a CRM system will get done, especially if they are drop down boxes and you don't have to think too hard.

Sales methodology

A sales methodology is a process that will guide you from initial meeting to final close. So why, you might ask, am I writing a book on one if there are many that already exist? Good point. In my view all of these systems miss the target. They are designed for the wrong type of salesman, the one who loves processes, detail, and loads of forms to fill in. Well, I struggled with this, as I am sure most of you will - so what this Ace the Sale methodology is about, is taking some of the best sales methodologies but overlaying them with my own sales experience and things that get missed from these rigid processes.

Most importantly the whole process needs to be fun. If you enjoy using a CRM system you will use it better which in turn will help you to win more business. The methodology is also designed to lay out a roadmap where you (and your team) can accurately determine how far into a sale you are. One measure of this book's success is when your sales manager next reviews an account with you and says: "What hole are you on? Are you on the back nine yet, or are we off to the 19th?"

Miller Heiman

I have been on many sales training courses over the years. Without doubt my recommendation for a great sales methodology would be *Miller Heiman*'s. They were the first company to really look at selling as a profession, and made their name in the late 1980s with numerous leading software and hardware companies. There are other sales methodologies that purport to offer something different but in my opinion they are all based around Miller Heiman's principles.

Since the company's early success, they have kept up to date, offering new releases of their books and training courses. Although there is a lot of hype about Sales 2.0 (which I will discuss later when we get further around the course) - Sales 2.0 is *not a sales methodology*. It is a way of generating business for companies that sell a commodity, and it is a lead generation tool for companies that need a direct sales force.

Miller Heiman offers a number of sales methodologies such as conceptual selling, large account management, and strategic selling to name a few. Strategic selling is the 'one to use' in software, services or major capital goods sales as it lays out the process of qualifying a deal, and how to manage it right through to the close - the backbone of any sales campaign.

By having a consistent methodology in your company, everyone speaks the same language and management knows where they stand with a sales rep when using terms such as: red flags, coach, win win, in the funnel, best fit, economic buyer, etc.

It's like having the best clubs on the market, the caddie that has done all the work mapping out the course, and the best golf coach so your swing will not break under pressure coming down the 18th... when you need a four to win!

One of the key concepts in Miller Heiman is to identify the best sales opportunities before you even start a sale. For example if you were selling an ERP system it might be:

- My best prospect is one that is in trouble, losing market share, and who needs a new ERP system to reduce stock and improve shipments to customers. There is a budget for this and the whole company is committed to installing a new system.

How many times are we chasing the wrong deal right from the very start?

Miller Heiman also utilises a *review approach* called a blue sheet that flags up weaknesses and strengths in the bid for an account. It is vital to know where you are weak, and not just strong, as it means that you can do something about it. For example, sales reps can often make the mistake that whenever they struggle to talk to one of the influencers in a sale – they just avoid speaking to them.

> My tip is always this – sell to the people who say NO, and manage the people who say YES.

If you are not turning the No(s) into Yes(es), and the No(s) are more influential, then you have probably qualified the deal badly and you need to get off the course and back to the clubhouse as quickly as possible to find another golf course that you can play.

Who are we dealing with?

There will be a number of people involved in the buying process in any complex sale. Most people resist change and will have their own agendas that need to be uncovered.

Miller Heiman identifies these people as:

- *User Buyers*: the people that will use the product, or receive the service.
- *Technical Buyers*: the people who look into the technical implications of buying your solution.
- The *Economic Buyer*: the person who signs the order or gives permission for the order to be signed off.
- The *Coach*: the inside person who will guide you through the sales process from the prospect's end. A general rule is that if you have no coach then you have no deal.

I will add another buyer who I call the *Anti-coach*. It is the anti-coach who is helping the other side (your rivals) to win; this person has to be handled very carefully and needs to be neutralised in the sale. It's the guy who shouts "Get in the hole!" at the top of your backswing, but whilst in most golf tournaments he is removed from the course – he is unlikely to be removed here.

If you can *turn* an anti-coach then most of the time you should win the deal. However if you can't turn them, you need to minimise their influence by showing other people on the team that your solution is the best and that the anti-coach's judgment is poor.

Normally you will only have one coach, although if you are really doing well two or three might surface, as well as one anti-coach and an economic buyer. There will be a number of user buyers and technical buyers.

Economic Buyer

Coach

Anti-coach

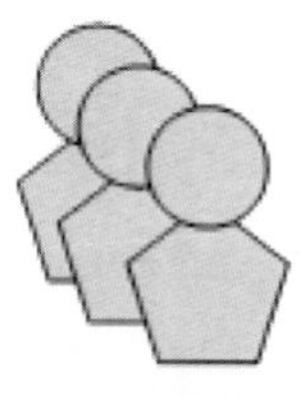

Technical Buyers

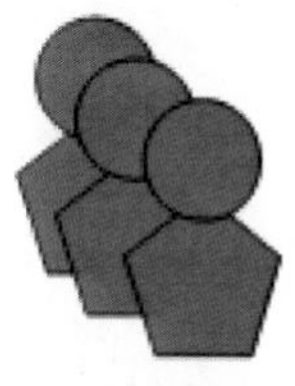

User Buyers

They will all have needs, fears and political issues with other staff members. Internal politics is something sales reps might not pay attention to but it's critical in a sale as you will see later down the course. If you are winning a deal then the anti-coach is losing and is therefore being isolated by the group. The chances are that when your solution goes in - they will be marginalised or looking for another job.

The Miller Heiman blue sheet highlights all these issues. By completing it you will realistically know where you are in the sale and you can form an action plan on what you need to do next. The blue sheet is available in Excel and integrates with some of the leading Customer Relationship Management (CRM) systems. But as I said upfront I would rather embed the sales process directly into the CRM system to make it easy for the sales rep to follow.

Customer Relationship Management (CRM) systems

CRM systems were born out of Sales Force Automation Systems and herein lays a problem. These systems are now so powerful and all-encompassing that they cater for every aspect of a business. They are becoming (in effect) a fully blown Enterprise Resource Planning (ERP) system. It's an obvious step that the CFO would want to get in on the act and have a single system for sales, support and accounting but in my opinion products that seek to handle everything will let the sales rep down badly on sales functionality - so I would avoid them. Buy a CRM system that is proven in the role of helping the sales rep and spend a bit of money on a programmer to carry out some interface work.

ERP systems should not be confused with bona fide CRMs designed for sales.

Having sold financial, distribution and manufacturing systems from the early 1980s – it is clear how the timescales from sale to implementation and ROI have changed over the years. Before integrated systems evolved, it used to take three months to install financial software (AP, AR and GL) then a further 6 months to add on distribution (SOP, POP, Inventory), and a further 12 months if you wanted manufacturing (MRP).

All of these systems are now fully integrated and are called ERP systems that can easily take two years to install. Unfortunately, when deployed inappropriately they can defocus the company on 'what they do', and at the end of the process the company struggles to produce a real return on investment.

This is the problem with too many CRMs - they want to be ERP systems; they try to do too much and take forever to install. In the meantime you will notice that the accounts, distribution, sales and manufacturing departments are all busy working away on spreadsheets.

Shadow systems: the hybrid club

If you are a sales rep working in a major multinational company that has one of the big CRM systems installed, I can guarantee you are only putting in the data that your boss needs, nothing more. Imagine this, you have just had a great meeting with one of the user buyers and you enter all of his details into the corporate CRM system. The next week he gets an email from a different division of your company trying to sell him something he does not want, or worse still there is a competitive product in your own company that is being pushed. How is he going to feel about that? So, in reality, you are not going to record key information anywhere but on your PC's local drive. I'll bet there is a spreadsheet with all the information that you require to run your sales campaign. Lo! A new CRM system for sales is born. The most important data for the sales cycle is hidden from corporate IT, the main CRM system, your colleagues and your boss.

Interestingly, the most successful implementations of software are when management do it under the radar of IT. These systems are called Shadow Data Systems (http://en.wikipedia.org/wiki/Shadow_system) and are everywhere in corporate life. Because ERP systems and CRM systems take so long to install and do not always meet the needs of the end user, the user takes the law into their own hands.

So what's my point? Well if you are playing golf you don't need to know how to play tennis. If you want to be the best golfer you need to focus and you need a CRM system that is flexible and customizable, which can be installed in a couple of months and which is designed for the sales team.

If you have been given the clubs to play with by your company and they are not the best, then you will go out and buy a hybrid club or two; you may want to keep this quiet as hybrid clubs risk upsetting the boss, especially if he follows the corporate line. Remember the first bit of professional advice from the Preface?

1. Always make sure that your boss is happy

If you use hybrid clubs – be careful!

Who to use?

If you have a choice of CRM system - then at the time of writing, Salesforce.com would be my recommendation. As the name suggests, this product was written for sales first and foremost. Furthermore, it's really easy to use and you can get something up and running in a month. Getting your data ready is key, but with Salesforce you can switch on additional modules, of which there are many, when (and if) you want them. So effectively you can take your time.

When I worked at The GL Company - we were struggling to get a well-known CRM system to work. We bit the bullet and switched to Salesforce, and within a month we had something useable which we built upon over time.

One of the great things about Salesforce is the ability to build new fields easily into the contact, lead and account fields. In fact, you can do this with any of the modules. It was through this customization facility that I incorporated Miller Heiman's methodology.

In the contact file I built categories and new text fields to hold further information. They included:

- What type of buyer I was dealing with.
  - Coach, Anti-coach, Economic Buyer, etc?

- How much time I had spent with them.
  - High, Medium, Low.

- What were their 'wins' out of this deal?
  - e.g. "Do they want to have experience of SaaS (Software as a Service) on their CV?"

- Were they on my/our side?
  - Yes, No, Don't Know, Neutral.

- Is the buyer struggling to do their job with their current system so they are 'open to change'? Or do they see no issues with the current solution they have, so won't want to buy? What mode are they in?
  - Panic, Trouble, Even Keel, Don't Care, Over confident.

In the opportunities module I added:

- Do they have a compelling event? Something that they really need to do which compels them to buy your solution, like moving off a mainframe system on a particular date, and therefore a need to replace their software and hardware?

I also added a closing tab check list:

- Is pricing done and approved?
- Has the contract been sent way ahead of time for review?
- Is there a legal or buying department which can slow down the close?
- When is the board presentation?
- When is the board meeting to approve the solution?
- Who will sign the contract, and will they be in on that day?

I added many more fields that a great sales rep would know automatically but which an average sales rep might miss. We'll pick these up as we go around the course. A sales rep needs to be completely on top of his brief. What I was able to do at The GL Company was to turn a bunch of very good presales people into one of the best sales forces by *building in processes for them*.

In effect the sales team all had the same swing, and hit the ball straight down the middle.

What happens if you have no choice?

This is probably the norm. You already have a methodology and a CRM system, and it is not Salesforce.com. Well, this book's methodology has been designed to work hand in hand with any sales methodology so you just need the CRM system to be able to add a field called "hole" and be able to enter the number 5 to 19 - when the selling begins. But if you can't add fields or no one is willing to do this for you then you are going to have to utilise Outlook which is really a mini CRM system on its own (if you know how to use it) and Excel, or even another CRM system under the radar like Sugar CRM.

Sugar is an open source CRM system that I use for small to medium size businesses when their budget is low. In effect you will need a few hybrid clubs.

Summary

You would not play golf with hickory shafts, feather balls, or without a course planner, distance markers or a caddie. Hole one is all about getting the right equipment or training in place for the round ahead. Get this right and the forthcoming holes will be easier to play. Get it wrong and you will be taking double and treble bogies along the way, putting yourself into a losing position before you have reached the turn. The key points you need to take from this hole are:

- Having a sales process will enable everyone to communicate and know exactly where you are in a sales cycle.

- Having a great CRM system will enable you to incorporate these sales processes and help you close business. It will also enable management to really see the value that is in the pipeline.

- If you work with an inflexible CRM system you will need to buy a few hybrid clubs, and use Outlook and spreadsheets.

We can now head to the 2nd hole, and see what makes a great sales person!

The 2nd hole

Emotional Intelligence

You have just played a round of golf with the most boring person at the club. The conversation was all about him and you hope that you never get paired with him again. Compare that with the four-ball that has just finished where there is laughter and everyone is having a good time. This is down to Jimmy who is the most likeable person at the club; he just seems to get on with everyone. Why is it that some people are better than others at people skills? Is it down to their level of Emotional Intelligence? What is Emotional Intelligence? Can you learn it, or are you just born with it?

On this hole we will cover

- The definition of Emotional Intelligence (EQ).
- What you can do about it if you are low on EQ.
- Empathy; understanding other people's hidden emotional drives.
- Neuro-Linguistic Programming – simplified for sales people.
- Body Language, and why it's so important.

What is Emotional Intelligence?

Emotional Intelligence has two aspects:

1. Understanding yourself, intentions, emotional responses and behaviour.
2. Understanding others, their feelings, their wants and expected behaviour.

You can soon get lost when you start reading books on this subject. Indeed, once you have read them you might end up knowing the theory, but not how to use EQ in practical terms. The books spend so much time discussing the *what* and the *why*, they miss out on the *how*. How can you discover your EQ? And how to find out other people's EQ? I am going to address these issues on this hole.

> My definition of EQ for salespeople:
> EQ enables you to maximize your own sales potential by firstly understanding yourself and then understanding how other people are made up - enabling you to communicate in a way that they would like, rather than from your point of view.

Emotional Intelligence is known as EQ which for the dyslexic people out there (of which I am one) does cause some confusion but highlights the recognition that EQ and IQ are similar; one is a measure of intelligence and the other a measure of the emotions.

Emotional Intelligence is more important than IQ

Research shows that EQ in a commercial environment may actually be significantly more important than information processing abilities and technical expertise combined. In fact, some studies indicate that EQ is more than twice as important as standard IQ abilities. Furthermore, evidence increasingly shows that the higher one goes in an organization, the more important EQ can be. For those in leadership positions, Emotional Intelligence skills are believed to account for close to 90 percent of what distinguishes outstanding leaders from those judged as average. IQ gets you hired, but EQ gets you promoted.

So what makes a great sales person and can EQ help?

I am sure you have heard many times people referring to someone as 'a natural'. Or that someone can 'sell fridges to Eskimos'. These sales people have great people skills or EQ; they are in tune with peoples' emotions, body language and can read people. It's a gift. Like playing great golf.

I can remember when I was working in presales on an account. When we finished the presentation the sales guy said to me:

"That went well, don't you think?"

Went well!?! It was terrible, people were looking at their watches, there were no questions, and we really had not understood the client's issues as we spent most of the time telling them how great we were. I could not understand how he could have come away from the same presentation with such a different point of view. We were clearly in trouble, and needed to do some serious rethinking if we were going to win the account.

The difference between the sales guy and me was in gauging how the pitch went. He had not tuned in to the unspoken signals that the people in the room were giving out.

Almost everyone at a pitch will be polite and tell you the meeting was a positive one, and that they can see good things ahead, but is this verbal reassurance backed up by the other signals they give out? If you can't pick up on these signals - you won't win many accounts, and sales will be a short career.

On the tee

We were setting up an agent network in Singapore and were asked to do a presentation to a prospective agent and their staff.

The sales guy spent an hour talking enthusiastically about the company and the products, he told his funniest jokes but not a single laugh (let alone a word) came from the audience. After he had finished he asked if there were any questions, no one said a word, no one moved. Hurriedly he went over to his sponsor and said "How did that go? They were all so very quiet."

"Yes," replied the sponsor. "Unfortunately no one speaks English."

True story.

It's all about course management - some golfers adapt to the circumstances and know when to take an iron off the tee, whilst others blaze away with the driver and consistently hook the ball out of bounds.

Here is one more

We were presenting to the CEO of a Japanese Bank and I was doing the presales. The salesman did not ask how long he had to speak, and after we had done the presentation he just went on and on and on. Japanese culture is such that it is rude to just get up and leave so the CEO stayed on and was late for a far more important meeting. No wonder we did not win this deal.

Adapting one's persona

For me 'people skills', as it was called at the time, came early as I was brought up in a pub called the Bottle and Glass, between Aylesbury and Thame, in the South of England. My Grandparents had the Bugle Horn just down the road and they did hot food whilst my parents specialized in cold table. My Grandparent's pub got overbooked most days and they would recommend the Bottle, and it was not long before my parents had a thriving business with all the local companies coming in for lunch.

As a teenager I used to help out in the bar. One moment I would be discussing how I wanted to become a chartered accountant with the chairman of Rothmans, and the next moment I would be serving the village idiot in the public bar listening to jokes he made up.

"Nick," said Jack. "What happens if you dropped a nail in the Red Sea?"

"Hold on a minute Jack, I just need to serve the chairman of Rothmans a gin and tonic. I will be back with you in a minute… Right Jack. What was the joke again? Oh yes I remember something about a nail, sorry I just don't know."

"Nothing," was his reply.

"Nothing?"

"Yes. Nothing. Because you would lose it."

Jack never made up any good jokes; I bet you have never heard that one before.

My point here is that I constantly had to adapt and change my personality to suit whoever I was serving. I did not realize it at the time, but I was picking up valuable EQ skills at a young age.

We were also fortunate to have a great local trade and on Friday night we had barristers, accountants, sales managers, engineers and a number of self-made multi-millionaires. So by the time I was ready to start my business career I felt that I had met most types of people which meant that I could adapt. The only problem was that I had decided to become a chartered accountant and that required a 'particular' personality. None.

Anyway, I started my training as a chartered accountant, and can remember one day when I was working in the audit room. Another articled clerk had just joined and, like me, was probably doing the wrong job. We got on well and were talking as we worked. At that point the audit manager came in and split us up – no talking! My new colleague had to go to the library to work. How I got through 5½ years in that business I will never know.

It was around this time that I was playing my best golf. I had managed to win two club championships in a row which allowed me to daydream, hoping that one day I could turn pro and leave the world of debit and credit. But my escape from audit and accounting was close… I was about to discover another world. A world in which having a personality was very important.

No EQ. What can you do?

So, if you have not got terrific natural EQ, or not had the good fortune to be brought up in a pub, what can you do to become a great sales rep?

Well the next best thing is to learn how to deal with people. When I was working as the UK sales director for JD Edwards our area Vice President at the time persuaded me to take a look at a sales course called 'Empathy Selling'. I was in my mid 30s at the time, and one thing at that age is that you think you know it all; no you don't think - you know you know it all!

Since I have retired from corporate work to run my own video and marketing company I have read more books on business than I ever did when I was younger. Books that *would* have made me even better. You never stop learning, and anyone who has bought this book and gets to the end, should hopefully pick up some tips and tricks that they did not know beforehand and will become a better sales person. It's the guys who stop learning and acquiring information who will carry on making mistakes; these are the 10 to 13 handicap golfers that never get to single figures because they refuse to take a lesson or two.

In the same way that it's always a good thing to go see your golf pro from time to time as errors can creep into your game, it's a good idea to buy some books on selling or go on new courses. You are never too old to learn.

Anyway we started the 'Empathy Selling' training and it was simply amazing, it was like a light had gone on. This was the answer as to why I could communicate better than other sales people. I had been subconsciously trained over the years in the pub to react to different personality styles.

What Empathy Selling did was to offer a personality framework. A framework that broke people down into 7 core emotions.

1. *Hustler:* Desire for money.
2. *Normal:* Desire for social approval.
3. *Mover:* Desire for communication.
4. *Double-Checker:* Desire for security.
5. *Artist:* Desire to be creative.
6. *Politician:* Desire to win.
7. *Engineer:* Desire to complete projects.

Now, most people typically have two or three dominant emotions, as well as a balancing emotion (the normal).

You can work out what type of person someone is just by observing their behaviour, how they dress, the car they drive, the position they hold in a company, their office layout, how they talk, and whether they keep you waiting for an appointment.

I used this framework extensively at JD Edwards and later at The GL Company where we added all these fields into the CRM system so that when I reviewed an account I could quickly see what type of personality any prospect was.

Empathy Selling is the missing link and in my view should be included in all books written on EQ as it explains HOW to find out your core emotions and the emotions of other people.

Sell to the personality as much as the person

People 'like' people who are similar to themselves. Therefore adapt your approach for your audience:

- If you sell to an *Engineer* give them detail.
- *Artists* need technical and design features - ask them to imagine the benefits so they can dream.
- *Movers* want the big picture, and they want it quickly.
- *Politicians* don't want to back down, so you need to sell slowly and influence them indirectly so *they* come up with the idea.
- *Double Checkers* need security; they need to be confident that they won't lose their job if they buy from you.
- *Normals* want references.
- *Hustlers* want a discount and the names of prestigious companies that use your product or services.

> If you are a manager, Empathy Selling can also be used to help you recruit sales reps. In the appendix, there are 21 questions that will score the traits above.
>
> Incidentally, the best profiles for sales reps are high scoring numbers for Hustlers, Movers and Politicians. You do get the occasional Engineer that can sell, but they will need high Mover and Politician scores in their dominant traits.

Combining Miller Heiman with Empathy Selling

What's really interesting is when you combine the types of personalities listed above with Miller Heiman's types of buyers. IT staff, for example, will normally be Engineers / Double Checkers, they need detail and reports to make decisions. But if you meet an IT person that shows little engineering quality (in terms of personality), then they might be struggling in their role and internal politics could be rife as they try to hold down their job, or rely on bluff and bluster to get by.

As mentioned on the previous hole, one of the most important Miller Heiman buyers is the Coach. Time for an anecdote…

On the tee

I can remember an occasion when one of my sales team was really pleased with himself after coming back from the 19th with one of his prospects declaring that he had found the Coach in the deal and that the Coach was helping us. However, once we ran the personality test, we found out that our Coach was very likely to be a Mover (someone that always starts things, speaks to everyone, but rarely finishes anything). We quickly deduced that this person was likely to also be helping our competition as well as us. We altered our strategy accordingly, found another coach and won the deal.

> The best Coach is actually a Politician. Someone who wants their own way, who has authority, and who has the motivation to get things done. It's this element that Miller Heiman and other sales processes miss.

Further reading

Today there are many books on the subject of EQ and sales. One of the first books was written back in 1937 by Dale Carnegie: *How to win friends and influence people*. It is just as valid a read today as it was then.

One of the first personality tests came out two years before Carnegie's book, the *Humm-Wadsworth Temperament Scale personality test* (1935). There is also the Myers-Briggs Type Indicator (MBTI) Assessment, and the DISC model of personality profiling. In many ways, a lot of the core philosophies behind these tests can be encapsulated under the umbrella of Emotional Intelligence (EQ).

There are hundreds of books on EQ, the most popular being *Emotional Intelligence* by Daniel Goleman which has sold over 5 million copies.

I might not totally agree with everything that people claim about EQ, but one thing is for sure - most sales reps will not want to read the mountain of information as it's aimed at Engineers, Artists, Double Checkers and Normals. As I mentioned above, the best profiles for sales reps are high scoring numbers for Hustlers, Movers and Politicians.

I will be referring to these personality traits throughout our round. *Empathy Selling* by Chris Golis is a must read for all sales reps as it short and easy to read. I was so impressed with this book that Chris and I have done a joint venture on the republishing of it. You can find more information on *www.EmpathySelling.com*.

Neuro-Linguistic Programming (NLP)

So Empathy Selling identifies the 7 core emotions and we know to adapt our sales mode to support the characteristics that these personality types represent. But this is not enough to build great EQ. NLP, which has its advocates (and which has its sceptics), fills in the gaps but it is a massive topic and again there are hundreds of books out there. When you start to read them you may get confused as it is so all-encompassing.

As with most things, there are 'elements' of NLP that can help sales people, and my take on NLP is this:

- It will help you to present and communicate better by understanding how people are hardwired to receive and compute information.
- It will help you look at sales situations from other people's points of view.
- It will help you to concentrate on people's faces when you talk to them which gives the impression that you are interested in what they are saying.
- It will help your confidence, ahead of an important meeting or presentation.

Whether NLP offers validated insight into human behaviours and functioning is a moot point. Sales people need to use what works, and I shall run through what I have seen to work at the sales coalface.

How people are hardwired

When we are born, we are hardwired to receive information in three predominant ways, and people will have a preferred means of acquiring information.

1. *Visual.* These people want to see things in pictures, so will switch off if there is loads of text and written material.
2. *Kinaesthetic.* More touchy feely people who want pick up a report, or want to use your product or service as part of the demo.
3. *Auditory.* These people learn by listening and are easily distracted by noise. They like reading but find writing difficult, as they are better at telling.

These definitions can fit most people, and if we look to combine what the three categories above tell us, with a bit of Empathy Selling we can see that Movers and Artists, for example, will normally be visual. Engineers and Double Checkers are often Kinaesthetic. Movers, Politicians and Double Checkers will be auditory.

> *My* point here is that whenever you do a presentation you need to ensure that you are communicating in all three ways. Never have a slide presentation just full of words as the Visual people won't respond to this. Conversely don't have a presentation that is just pictures - you will leave the Auditory and Kinaesthetic people cold. Your presentations need to offer a bit of everything.

When we did pitches I would make sure that we had hand-outs during the presentation especially for the kinaesthetic people. It was so interesting to see how these people used hand-outs. They didn't really read them at the time but they did like to 'flick' through them, and it adds substance to a presentation. *Don't leave hand-outs on the table* to give out at the end - as the kinaesthetic people will want to get their hands on them as soon as possible and will feel frustrated during the presentation.

A good example of using all 5 of the senses (we have only covered 3: Sight/Visual, Sound/Auditory and Touch/Kinaesthetic) is in real estate in the US. Realtors/Estate Agents know the tricks of the trade. When there is an open house viewing - you will go into a property and there will be some soft background music (hearing) and a coffee pot on the go with a lovely aroma (olfactory/smell, that's a new sense) and you might be invited to taste one of the lovely cookies on the kitchen counter (gustatory/taste, the last of the 5). The agent will ask people to physically feel things like door handles, surfaces (for quality) and get purchasers to *look closely at* particular features. It's a multimedia experience!

There are always three sides to every situation

The biggest mistake that sales people make is making decisions based on *their own agenda and standards.* People invariably judge people by their own standards, however we are all different.

On the tee

We were closing a deal using a Microsoft Word document when we got stuck on one point. We could not move on it as it was non-negotiable from our side, and the client agreed to go forward. Later, as we were about to sign the contract one of the buying team stopped me from signing.

"Nick, the IT manager has changed one of the clauses without your permission and I am not happy with this," he said.

Now it had never even crossed my mind that the IT manager would do this - because this is something I would never do. I had applied my own standards to the situation and could have come a cropper. So, we subsequently developed a protocol to prevent this happening again and used PDFs from then on which, at the time, were difficult to change.

On other occasions, we caught customers having many more users of our software than in the contract. We eventually had to build software to check the number of users as the contract did not protect us from misuse.

What I am trying to say here is that people behave differently, and using techniques (such as those offered by NLP) can help you get into the mind of other people, and how they react; not how *you* would react. I have found that a Hustler with low Normal will often try to bend the rules, whereas a regular Normal will play everything with a straight bat.

The three positions that NLP teaches you are:

- *1st position.* This is your perspective of what is happening.
- *2nd position.* Take the perspective of the person you are talking to.
- *3rd position.* A fly on the wall who is observing the conversation or action in a detached manner.

Human beings are amazing. Whatever you say, however right it is, there will always be someone who will think the opposite.

When you are working on a deal, it will pay dividends to use the *3 position technique*. It won't take long. Sit down for 10 minutes with a pad of paper, and list what you would experience from each position. Actively look for differences between the three positions. On a typical deal it might look as basic as this.

Position 1: I want to earn some commission.

Position 2: The buyer wants something on their CV that will help them to get a better job.

Position 3: The sales guy just wants money and the buyer is out for himself.

Action: You need to make sure you do not come across as though all you want is the commission. Find a way that the buyer will get some perceived value to his job prospects if he selects your product.

Once, we had a UK agent and the CEO was a very interesting character, no-one could work him out. In the end, I developed a rule of thumb for dealing with him. I said to my sales team:

"Think what a rational person would do and then expect the opposite."

The fact that he was inscrutable was not really an issue. We identified what we thought he was like, and developed a strategy for working with him.

Everyone lies to you

One thing I instilled in all my sales teams is that everyone lies to you, and you never get a straight answer. It's not that people are dishonest; it is just that people don't like confrontation and are happy for you to go on believing whatever you wish. So when someone says they will buy the product, I don't get excited until I get confirmation from another party. The more parties the better, but as a sales rep - don't rely on what you hear. Find out for yourself.

Focus on people's eyes

Now let's get into the nitty gritty of face-time.

> Listen to what people are saying, and show that you are listening. Use your ears and mouth in the same proportion that you were born with. Twice as much listening as talking.

How often do you see an iPhone or Blackberry go off with a text message and the person you are talking to starts to read it? Are they listening to you? Of course not. A sales rep has to focus on the prospect every time, and a least give the impression that they are listening even if they are boring you to death. It feels unnecessary to say it, but I am going to say it anyway. When you are with a prospect, switch off your phone and focus on them. If they choose to look at text messages, there is nothing you can do. But at least *you* are acting properly.

Now a really fun thing about NLP is that your eyes move to certain spatial zones when you are asked questions that relate to pictures, sounds and feelings. Ask someone you know the following questions and watch where their eyes go.

- *What does your best friend look like?* Eyes will go up to the right to the visualizing remembered images zone.
- Ask a question that they will **not** know the answer to, but which they feel they should. *What colour is your next door neighbour's front door?* Eyes will go up to the left which shows visualizing, constructing an answer, or in other words - making it up.

- Ask a question about a sound they know - like *what does Kermit the Frog's voice sound like?* Eyes will go to the central right 'remembering sounds' zone.
- Now a question about sound that they don't know. *What would Kermit's voice sound like if he impersonated Miss Piggy?* The respondent's eyes should now go to the centre left (auditory constructing sounds).
- Ask a question about feelings. *What does it feel like when you dive into a cold swimming pool?* Eyes will go to the kinaesthetic, checking out feelings zone, down to the left.
- Ask them to recite the 12 times table in their mind. Eyes will go to kinaesthetic internal dialogue down to the right.

The above eye pattern movements are for a person who is normally organised. Around 20% of people are actually *reverse* organised which means that everything is swapped around. So recall would be looking to the left rather than to the right. You need to check this out when you first meet a prospect and ask some simple questions that will inform you how they are organised.

"How was your journey to our office this morning?" you might ask. Watch the eye movement especially if there was a traffic jam or something relevant that they would need to recall. As you engage in small talk, take note of eye movements and determine if your prospect is normally or reverse organised.

The following illustration maps out the zones discussed (normally organised). Note how one side is all about constructed perceptions, and the other is all about recall. If there is a lot of eye movement to the left then this could indicate to you that your prospect is making up things on the fly, which should make you suspicious. Although I would never advocate asking how things are going in a sale (after all - "if you don't know you are winning then you are losing!") but just imagine what would happen if you asked this question.

"So Bill you have been working with us now for over 5 months. What's your take on things? Would you buy our product?" Then say nothing. I think you would be pretty interested in where the eyes go when he answers this one.

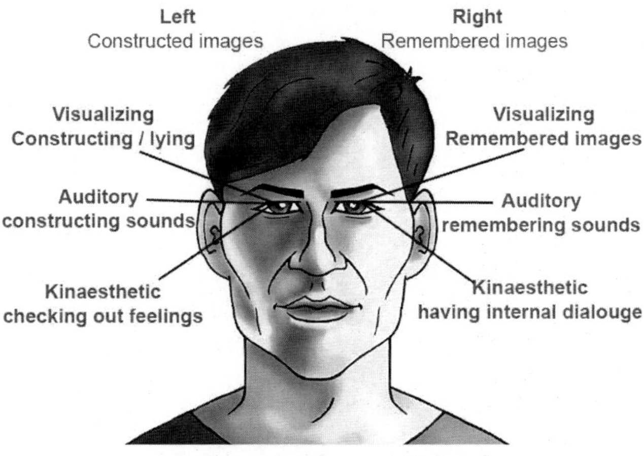

Eyes position as looking at another person

Building confidence, anchoring

Anchoring is where you can recall a mind state (such as a very positive experience) through a physical action, which then takes you back to the experience so that you feel it again, e.g. feeling confident ahead of a presentation or an important meeting. It is extremely powerful in helping you to have more confidence and enthusiasm (even fun) when meeting people.

When you create an NLP anchor you set up a stimulus response pattern so that you can feel the way you want to, whenever you need to, in response to a particular stimulus.

With sales, it is useful to bring about a particular emotional state whenever you need it. This is how it is done.

1. Identify the emotional state you want, e.g. confidence, calmness, enthusiasm.
2. Select a desired state, i.e. *specifically* how you want to feel.
3. Recall a particular time in your life when you felt the desired state. Pick a powerful example. Try to remember this situation and think how it was building up to the moment. If you can't think of anything from your past, think of a film or some music that makes you feel the way you want. Eye of the Tiger, anyone?
4. Now you need to anchor this feeling by putting it onto one of the knuckles on your hand. When you need it, just touch the knuckle, and replay the event/sound/memory in your head.
5. Practise and rehearse until it becomes second nature.

Confidence is such an important component for Sales. Confidence breeds success, and I buy into the idea that "if you are frightened to fail, then you will never succeed". In other words – be confident and do not worry unduly about the flip side... failure.

On the tee

At the Bottle and Glass pub, I once got chatting with one of the most successful businessmen that came in regularly. He was a multi-millionaire back in the early 1970s and I asked him:

"How did you make your money?"

He replied. "Business is simple," You buy something for 50p and sell it for £1 and you make 50p profit. Business does not get any harder that that but just has more zeros attached to it."

He had such a simple outlook on things and made me realise that business was not hugely complicated. These words *really* stuck with me, and gave me confidence, to the extent that I am not frightened to have a go at anything. So my anchor is recalling the businessman's words. Everything is simple - it's people that make things complicated.

Body language

Body language really tells you what someone is actually thinking and most people can't disguise it. If what your prospect says is contradicted by their body language then they are not telling the truth. Unless you are an experienced fraudster it takes a lot of acting to disguise body language. For some people even the obvious signals get missed and in sales, if you can't read body language (and also remain aware of your own signals), you won't make it. Let me explain.

On the tee

I can remember a meeting in the US with a potential customer. Our head of sales in the US had come from a consulting background, whilst I was running worldwide sales and marketing at the time. We were just getting started in the US and had made some good progress.

At this particular meeting our head of sales knew the prospect well, but wanted to impress me. So he kicked off the meeting and after a while the prospect started to talk. No sooner had the prospect started to speak than our head of sales tried to jump right back in. His mouth was moving but no words were coming out. He was desperately looking for a way to interrupt the prospect but there was no opportunity to talk. Everyone could see that he was not paying attention. He was more interested in what *he* wanted to say.

Eventually he started to talk and talk and talk, and when the conversation got into full flow he started to point his finger at the prospect - moving it up and down. I was shocked and uncomfortable and was witnessing the worst case of body language I had ever seen.

He might as well have said:

"Hey! Mister Prospect! You are full of it. This is what you need to do. I know so, because I am right and you are wrong."

My sales colleague had been a really successful presales person with a great career to that point. But how do you tell someone at their age that their body language is terrible? How do you tell someone that unless they change their body language they won't have a job anymore?

This is when I decided to introduce a sales methodology and training course for *all* new sales people, especially as we had a philosophy of taking good presales people and turning them into great sales reps. Part of the training was on body language. So much of what you say does not come from your mouth but the signals that you give out from your body.

Here are some ground rules.

- Never interrupt a prospect when they are in full flow, a good meeting is them talking and you listening. Let the prospect empty out so that you can really understand their issues and concerns before you reply.
- Never wag your finger at anyone in a meeting. Keep your hands down in a neutral position.
- Always look interested and concentrate on their eyes so that you keep eye contact. However, some people like Artists won't like this, so adapt your behaviour. Make sure that if you are selling to this type of person you don't make them uncomfortable by looking in the eyes too much.

Rapport between two people is defined as the ability to relate to others in a way that creates a climate of trust and understanding. When you communicate - only 7% is 'what you say', 38% is the tone that you use, and 55% is the physiology or body language that you give out.

On the tee

When I was running sales at JD Edwards – "Geoff" would always take me into a meeting and then completely dominate the sale. It was like playing a game of soccer where he was the striker, midfield, defence, and goalie. I never got the ball once.

I would desperately try to speak, but he did not notice my body language and just carried on talking. Unfortunately the prospect probably picked up on it but not my sales guy. So I used this analogy when we next went into a meeting. "Geoff, don't forget to pass me the ball now and again, and keep your eyes open on the manager's bench as he just might want to give you some instructions." Anyway, Geoff took this on-board, and we worked together very well from that point onwards. Never take someone into a meeting if you are not going to use them, otherwise leave them back at the clubhouse.

> Remember to tune into the body language of your colleagues as much as your prospects.

I can remember when Greg Norman collapsed in the last round of the 1996 Masters tournament. Norman started with a six stroke lead but began the round with a snap-hook bogey. On the other hand Faldo was the epitome of self-control. He set out to score a par on every hole and on the first four holes scored par-birdie-par-par. Norman started to fidget intensely and take an age over routine approaches. Anyone watching could see from the ninth hole onwards that Greg did not stand a chance. His body language was giving out the signals of defeat and lack of confidence for all of us to see. Norman ended up five strokes behind Faldo.

If you play golf you have probably been there yourself, and once confidence crumbles it's hard to recover. My take on this is that you are going to have to hit the ball no matter what - so you might as well have a positive thought in your head than a negative one. This is the time to look for your anchors and get back your composure and confidence.

Summary

People with high EQ don't have to work too hard on this hole but for most of us we can understand how people are made up by using Empathy Selling. Thinking about other people's points of view, watching eye movements and gaining confidence with NLP will make you more engaging and perceptive. Understanding body language will give you the tools to increase your EQ and make you a more interesting and successful sales person.

Now we know how to communicate with the prospect, we are ready to move on to hole 3 which is all about competition. It is one thing knowing how you will react in a sales battle, but if you don't know what your competition is going to do - then the chances of success diminishes. Onwards!

The **3**rd hole

Competition

Knowing your competition is just as important as knowing your own game. If you know how your competition is going to react - you can lay the foundations to a great sales cycle. What sales book worth its salt does not have a Sun Tzu quote? Here's a good one:

If you know the enemy and know yourself, you need not fear the result of a hundred battles. If you know yourself but not the enemy, for every victory gained you will also suffer a defeat. If you know neither the enemy nor yourself, you will succumb in every battle. Sun Tzu "The Art of War".

On this hole we will cover

- Why lost business is so important to future wins.
- Losing with dignity enables you to win another day.
- Is lost business buried in your company?
- Why the marketing department should dedicate time on lost business.
- The brown envelope.

Losing business

You will get to know your competition over time. Wins and losses will help you draw up a profile not just on how strong their products are, but the sales tactics they use. By winning a deal it becomes easy to get this information as your prospect is now your customer and friend, however the best market intelligence is when you lose a deal as you will see things from the perspective of someone who did not want your product or service rather than from a supporter. If you lose you need to lose with grace so that the prospect is willing to share this vital information with you and you learn from this experience. Plus, you should be able to keep the door open for the future.

On the tee

I hate losing, and early in my selling career when I was working for Insight Database Systems, we had the best product on the market; you did not have to be too good at selling then, provided you could demonstrate the product. However a new vendor had entered the market from the US and we had just lost our first deal to them. They had no users in the UK and the product was not as good as ours, so I wrote a letter to the project manager who was coordinating the sale to tell her why she was so stupid to buy this product.

This letter was the worst mistake I had ever made. Firstly, it got into the hands of the sales rep of the competition who then used it against me in future deals. Secondly, I had no debriefing as to why we lost the sale. Lastly, I could never sell to this company or person again which meant that if she left and joined another organisation our solutions would not even get on the shortlist.

This really hurt me as I felt so stupid, and from then on if I (or anyone on my team) ever lost a deal we would always lose with grace and get a debriefing from the prospect on why we lost. It is really important to understand that a debrief is not another opportunity to try and get back in. What you want are all the reasons why you lost, and an opportunity to build bridges for the future so that you can be considered by this buyer again.

You may have some sales people disagreeing with me here saying “When the prospect says ‘no’, this is where the selling starts”. Well, this might be okay on a one-to-one basis where you are selling double glazing to some poor old age pensioner, but not in a complex sale with multiple buyers. If you follow “Ace the Sale” you will see that if you have done your job correctly, all the selling is done before the decision is made (hole 16) not after!

Anyway the next time you want to write a letter to a prospect to tell them how stupid they are - write it and then bin it. It is very therapeutic but whatever you do - don’t put it in the post! The world is a very small place and what goes around comes around.

Just out of interest, the reason why we lost this deal was that the project manager was a personal friend of the CEO of the company that was representing the product in the UK. If I had employed a sales process, I could have done something about this, but we were just demo kids in those days and had no concept of what a sales process was.

Sometimes when you lose a deal, as you can see from the example above, you have probably lost it from the very beginning and this is why the first meeting is so important. We will be covering more of this on hole 5.

Is lost business getting buried?

Having just said how important lost business is to future business, it is surprising how little this topic is discussed at sales, management and board level. We tend to be defensive when things go wrong rather than holding our hands up and finding out why we really lost a deal.

By having a good sales process you will be able to see where you are in the sales cycle and any deal that gets to the 16th - that you end up losing - needs to be investigated and reported at management and board level.

The reason why lost business gets buried is that it is normally down to mistakes by the sales rep and management but in most companies people are fearful of admitting mistakes. Sales reps know when bad news is coming but struggle to be honest with their boss or indeed themselves about it in the hope that this bad news will somehow sort itself out on its own.

Getting bad news out of a sales rep is very hard and I recognised this issue. When I recruited a new person I would always say that you have 10 mistakes before I get worried. This was great as it took the pressure off and I got the truth about what was going on. Getting bad news early is good news as you can do something about it. This is all about having good quality sales management who engender an atmosphere where sales reps can share bad news rather than the "bully boy" school of sales management where no one wants to tell them any bad news; they just find out when the business is lost or never closes and by then they can't react.

So lost business is a reflection on the sales rep and management and it gets buried or justified. "Yes, I thought that we were doing okay, but they had no budget and we should not have gone for it". Having a sales process, as on hole 1, stops these justifications as this should have been qualified very early on in the sales cycle.

Competitive information - who owns it?

In most companies the detailed knowledge of a competitor will be in the heads of the sales rep. One sales rep might have valuable information on one competitor as they have competed many times with them, whereas other sales reps might not have ever come across them.

This information needs to be shared with the whole sales team and not reside in the heads of individuals, otherwise when they leave the company this competitive information will go as well.

On the tee

JD Edwards went public in 1997 and I can remember being on a European sales meeting and speaking to the then CEO at the time. "You know Nick, we are one of the fastest growing ERP software companies in the world and we have so little information on our competitors. Yes we know all the old favourite ones who we have been competing with us for ages but with open systems we are going to be competing with new and bigger companies. I am going to set up a dedicated team just to focus on our competition."

These words stuck with me to this day and the information provided was really useful. We had all this data published in our knowledge garden which we could download when we went into battle.

I am a strong advocate of the principle that marketing should report to sales and my take is that marketing should own competitive information and have someone responsible for compiling all this information.

The marketing department should spend time surfing your competitor's website in particular and the web in general for any information. Also marketing should be responsible for the debriefing of lost sales not the sales person that lost the deal. We shall be discussing this in far more detail on the 16th when the decision is made.

I am not a great believer in having too much information on a public website without capturing user information (e.g. the user's email address) as you will see on hole 9. But if your competition puts everything they have on their site then take advantage and download as much as you can. However, too much information is useless unless it is distilled.

What I would advocate is to have a number of PowerPoint presentations. A 60 second elevator pitch, and a 3-to-5 minute sales pitch from your competitor's point of view. Think about how you would sell against yourself from each of your major competitors and this will throw up some weaknesses from your end that you will need to counteract.

Discuss competition at sales meetings and always have it as an agenda point with a focus on a different competitor each month.

This type of information should then be read by (and be of use to) the sales team. For the Engineers and Normals out there (remember Empathy Selling: Movers, Hustlers, Politicians, Engineers, Double-Checkers, Artists and Normals) you may want to dive into the detail, but for most sales reps - keep all this information high level and to the point.

On the tee

At JD Edwards we were starting to win business against the market leader in ERP solutions for the IBM AS/400 (now the iSeries). The feedback we kept receiving was that we 'actually showed software', whereas our short list competitor talked concepts and showed slides. Every time we came up against them we would make an issue of showing real customer data in the demo, and we won every competitive bid from then on as they could not respond.

We soon took over the market leader position and as we moved to open systems we had our sights set on SAP. As a company grows, your competition changes and initially you will lose more deals than you win against new vendors - until lessons have been learnt and the research has been done.

The brown envelope (dirt)

Knowing too much about your competition can backfire on you especially if it is in the hands of inexperienced sales people; they are much too eager to share information with anyone, whereas you have to use this information very carefully.

As on hole 2 (Emotional Intelligence), it is very important that you have earned the right to use competitive information. When you get further down the sales cycle and the players all start to make up their minds on which company they prefer, your coach is the only person that you need to supply the weaknesses of other vendors to, and only when they request it from you! Do not fall into the trap of badmouthing competition. If you don't get asked for it, you are probably losing the deal as the coach should be building up a case for why their company wants to buy from you. This information is what will form the basis of the decision, as well as the strengths of your product or service and users references.

Don't knock your competition. Focus on your strengths that show up the weaknesses of the competition. Let the prospect join the dots together for themselves and with a bit of help from your coach - bingo the lights will go on!

Summary

On this hole we have seen how lost business can lead to future wins provided you lose with grace which ensures that the door is still open to you in the future. Having as much information as possible on your competition will help you set out your sales strategy and even qualify 'out' of a deal if the competition is too strong.

With a sales process, a CRM system, Emotional Intelligence and detailed knowledge on your competition you are now ready to play the fourth hole: what's your sandwich? Find out why a low cost product can lead to bigger gains later on.

The **4**th hole

What's your Sandwich? Why Good Marketing Matters

Keeping your energy level high by having something to eat in your bag is essential during a round. But what has this got to do with selling?

Unless you are working for the market leader where the major consultancy firms and analysts are throwing leads at you, you just might need a low cost entry product to get into a new prospect. Something that I'll call a sandwich.

On this hole we will cover

- Why marketing should report to sales (part II).
- Why good relationships with consultants and analysts are essential.
- Having a low cost entry product will enable you to get in the door.
- Up selling is easier than finding a brand new customer.

Why marketing should report to sales

You have just joined a new company and have a $2m quota for the year. You are given your territory, an email account, and a new mobile phone. You have a high EQ and are one of the best sales reps around but there is one small problem, you don't have anything to bid on, and there are no leads to qualify. Whose responsibility is this?

Now this is going to be a very controversial hole as you will find many differing opinions here - but this is my take. If I put myself in the shoes of the sales manager for a moment, this is how I see things. I have just employed a sales rep to do a job, and that job is to:

- Qualify leads.
- Decide which accounts to bid on.
- Set realistic sales expectations.
- Run a professional and successful sales campaign leading to a new and happy customer.

Now to me that's a *big job*. A full time job. So how on earth are reps going to look for prospects as well?

When selling complex deals I would not want sales reps to be spending their time generating leads. A great marketing team is essential for feeding a sales force. I am a firm believer that the VP of sales should also be in charge of marketing. If someone gives me a big target but then says "you have no say in where you get your leads", it is like playing a round without distance markers, or a course planner, whilst carrying just 3 clubs and a putter. The player can't perform at his best and the sales rep can't deliver without good leads.

I have always taken charge of the marketing team as well as sales for this reason, and at JD Edwards my commitment to the sales team was "you run the sales cycle correctly, and I will get you the opportunities".

Most companies complain about the lumpiness of sales, one month it is high and another month there is nothing. If you are asking the sales rep to find business - this is what you get - a number of months prospecting followed by some semi focused sales campaigns with no time to prospect until they have either won or lost the accounts they are working on.

Whilst I appreciate that smaller companies might find themselves in this position it's a false economy and with today's CRM systems you can employ a bright young student to do email and telemarketing. The internet has also enabled us to do interactive demos and webinars online. More and more companies are employing inside sales departments to find leads and carry out the very first part of the sales qualification before the sales rep engages.

How many times (when you don't have sales running marketing) do you see the VP of marketing staying with a company for years but the VP of sales changing many times? The VP of marketing has to be more accountable if they are not reporting into sales, and both should succeed or fail together.

Marketing breakdown

Marketing can be split into three things:

1. Lead generation.
2. Market awareness.
3. Product marketing.

I am not intending to go into great detail on points 2 and 3, otherwise this hole would be a par 12 - so I want to focus on lead generation and highlight that successful selling depends upon successful lead generation. If you join a company that does not get this you won't succeed.

Lead generation not market awareness

In my view, too much of a marketing budget goes on market awareness. My focus is always on lead generation. At JD Edwards the majority of our leads came from consultancies. These were from the guys who were preparing the *Invitations To Tender* (ITTs) and advising companies on their IT strategy; if you were not covering them you just wouldn't get the leads.

We did really well with a number of the top consulting firms and we had many a golf day for the consultants to cement our relationship. There was however one firm that was totally dedicated to SAP and they had built a large team of consultants to install their ERP solution. Needless to say we ignored all ITTs from this firm.

IBM was another important source of leads at this time. With IBM and all the other relationships to look after, relationship management took up a great deal of my time. It was vital that I had a sales team that did not need babysitting so that I could concentrate on bringing them the opportunities. However I *always* attended the first meeting as you will see on the next hole.

Gartner

In the late 1990s, without a doubt the kingmaker for the ERP market was Gartner. Gartner today is one of the leading IT analyst firms and is widely followed by CIOs around the world. They have a graph called the Magic Quadrant (MQ, see over). If you make the top right hand quadrant you will get more companies interested in your products or services.

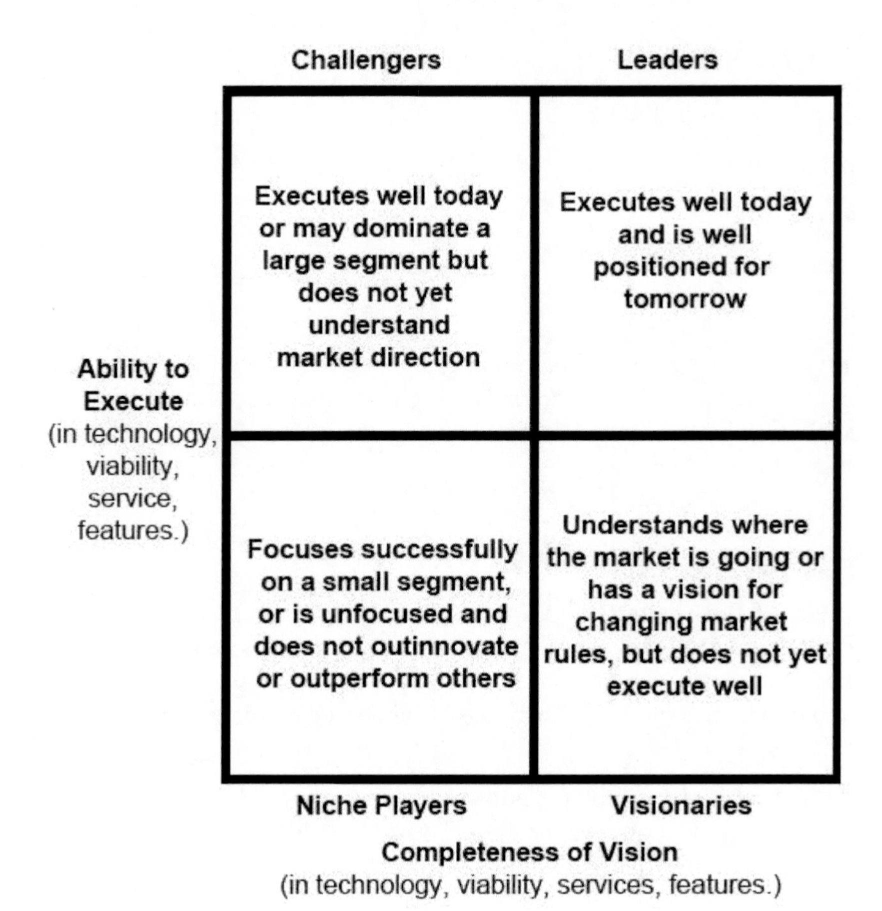

Source: Gartner

JD Edwards, at the back end of the nineties, without doubt had the best integrated ERP solution on the market because of the owner's strategy of building a common architecture for financials, distribution and manufacturing. What's my point here? Well in my opinion if we could have convinced Gartner at this time that we had integrated manufacturing software - JD Edwards might still have been an independent company today, or at the very least bigger than PeopleSoft at the time they acquired us.

We failed because we did not play the analyst's game. We had an analyst that was following JD Edwards and unfortunately we could not get our message across to him. There was a reason for this but I will not go into print as to why this was the case but the bottom line was we had a relationship issue. A bit more EQ on our part might have transformed our company.

They had the power and we were demoted behind PeopleSoft. How this could have happened from a software point of view was unbelievable. PeopleSoft had taken the opposite approach and bought various companies and interfaced them the best they could. You can normally tell when an ERP solution is not designed well if the use of a

Business Intelligence system has to be sold alongside. The reason for this is that it brings in all the different file structures that underpin a random ERP solution into one. Today one of the leading suppliers of ERP solutions has more Business Intelligence solutions than modules!

> If your company is not covering analysts and the big consultants well, it will impact upon your chances of success.

Having an entry level product is essential

If you are not fortunate in having the big consultants throwing you leads then you need to generate leads yourself. Throughout this book I will be talking about *earning the right* to say and do things. If you can sell a low cost product, and deliver a great solution and service - you *will* have earned the right to sell more. A worldwide deal for a product or service does not happen from day one, unless you happen to be the market leader and have the support of big consultancy firms. For most companies, however, selling sandwiches will get you to these deals.

Basing your marketing strategy on a good restaurant

Being the first European employee at JD Edwards meant that I chose where the office was going to be. Our first offices were in High Wycombe, but after a year we needed to find a better building. I managed to find a brand new 10,000sq foot office in Bourne End in Buckinghamshire. How on earth we were going to fill this I did not know, but Ed McVaney, the owner of JD Edwards (and who was working with us in the UK at the time), assured me that we were going to be big and that my job was to make sure that we grew out of the building in two years' time. Which we did.

We scouted around to find a nice pub to have lunch in, and to our delight we came across the Chequers Inn which was just up the road. It's an oldie worldie pub, with a roaring fire on your right hand side as you enter, low ceilings, antique furniture and a very friendly landlord to greet you. Just above the fire there was a hand written menu with various selections of sandwiches and pub lunches. Ed, coming from the US, fell in love with this place straight away.

We ordered some drinks and a few sandwiches which were reasonably priced. When they arrived we could not believe the quality and we complimented the landlord on them. "Thank you," he said. "They are from the same kitchen as our main restaurant around the back."

"What, you have a restaurant as well?" asked Ed.
We all went around to the back where we found this wonderful restaurant beautifully decorated.

We were back for dinner over the weekend and had a fantastic meal. The landlord showed us around the place before dinner as they had a few rooms and an annex where they did wedding receptions and functions.

As time progressed, we had many a meeting in this function room and soon became one of the pub's best customers. If fact you were more likely to get us at the Chequers Inn than at the office, and when Ed went back to the US he would regularly call the pub first if it was between 12.30 and 2.00 p.m. and 6.00 and 8.00 p.m. to get hold of us.

The pub was to become one of our closing techniques with prospects after an all-day demonstration. We would suggest to the key decision makers that they should come up for a quick drink before they set off home, to see this wonderful pub.

As soon as they got up there, the conversation changed from work to sport, and our competitors did not have a chance. Not only did we have the best product, we had a sales force with high EQ, and a pub that our prospects fell in love with.

So what's my point here - apart from having an office with a great pub down the road?

It's easier to up sell than to sell new business

What the landlord had successfully achieved was to get us to buy a sandwich which was well within our budget. This gave him an opportunity to up sell a much more expensive dinner, and then up sell us again on a function. I am sure that if any of us were getting married we would have probably bought a wedding reception.

> To sell a wedding reception, to someone you have never sold to, is hard, but to sell a sandwich to a stranger is easy.

At this time JD Edwards was selling standalone modules for financials, accounts payable, receivable and general ledger, which were not too expensive and easy to install. Soon we became the market leader in the financial area and when we launched the distribution modules we had a great user base to sell into.

Manufacturing followed and JD Edwards grew from $40m turnover in 1990 to over $1bn in just 8 years. JD Edwards went public in 1997 at a market capitalisation of over $3bn. We sold a lot of wedding receptions!

Do you have a sandwich?

If your company does not have a sandwich then you are probably a well-known company which has been trading for many years and are getting proposals and business from a great network. If you don't fit this profile then you need to start making sandwiches and getting a sales and marketing strategy to sell a low cost, low maintenance product.

This is something that you can bring up in a sales meeting to see if you can get development to build you one.

On the tee

At The GL Company we often sold a one user system for reporting – it was our sandwich. My first sale (in the first week I joined because I knew the CIO) was to a public manufacturing company. I called him up to see if we could help in anyway. "Our management accountant is pulling his hair out with reporting can you help?" he said.

I went up there, installed the product on his desk in 20 minutes, and straight away he started to use it. "Oh my God," he said, "we have had a variance on the TB for the last 5 years and I can now see the business unit that has the issue.

"Oh my God," he went on, as he found another issue that he could now solve. "What do you normally do about these issues I asked?"

"Oh we just roll them over to the next month as we need to get the reports out for the board, and we just don't have the time to find them," he replied. This took me back to my accounting days where I spent a whole week ticking the sales day book to the sales ledger to find 10 pence. No wonder I liked sales.

The noises coming from the management accountant's office attracted a few of his colleagues. "Can you have a look at this account for me?" one of them said. And it was not long before there were 4 people huddled around the screen all looking intently at the results our product was throwing up.

Needless to say we got a sale and over time we added more modules and up sold this customer. A small beginning led to a half a million dollar sale which continued to grow.

Most businesses will have spending limits at different levels of management and therefore you can normally get your first product into an account well under the radar of the purchasing manager or board. These first sales will lead to many more and you will also have a readymade coach in the company to promote your product for you.

I have sold many multi-million dollar deals but it was very rare to do one without one of the divisions of these accounts already having an installation of our software.

Twitter and Facebook

Today you can listen in on conversations that companies and people are having by setting up parameters to search on. For example if you install a product called TweetDeck you can set up columns that listen for anything anyone says about a certain @Vendor or #Subject in Twitter. A lead can be found when someone's frustration with trying to get a report out of JD Edwards tweets or Facebooks it out for the world to hear. If your marketing department is not doing this today, bring it up at your next sales meeting.

On the tee

Before we leave this hole I have to tell you this story. I have seen great marketing ideas, some come off and others backfire.

I had hired an Irish lady to help me in marketing when I was at JD Edwards. One of our guys in the US had come up with great idea. The idea behind selling integrated solutions was that everyone could interact with the data. The CFO has visibility of the CIO's data and the CEO has a view of everything. Integrated software gave a single version of the state of the business (if you ignore spreadsheets!).

Anyway the idea was this. Three parcels would be sent, one to each of the three guys above. We bought a remote controlled car and sent the car to the CIO, the Controller to the CEO and the batteries to the CFO with a note in each parcel to say that they must talk to their colleagues so that they can drive the car. Great idea you would think until we sent this to a local government department in Cheltenham at the height of the terrorist attacks.

The name on the letter was my assistant's. The next day she had a voice message that went like this.

Dear Miss O'Brien, never send any marketing material to our organisation again. In fact, never talk to us again as we would never consider your company in any capacity.

You parcels were intercepted by our security department and when x-rayed, they looked suspicious and we had to evacuate the whole building. All the staff were standing outside in the car park for over an hour until we discovered your stupid marketing idea. We will be writing to you headquarters about this.

Well, I bet they all knew who JD Edwards was now.

Summary

Holes 1 to 3 are vital but of no use to you if you don't have anything to bid on. This is why hole 4 is so important. You would not want to play a golf course that has bad fairways and greens and where it takes over five hours to play a round. It's the same for the company you work for, they need to maintain the course and give you a chance of being successful.

So next time you are on the course and you reach for your banana or energy bar think about your company and work out what your sandwich is. Is there something that can get you into a new customer? If you don't have one then speak to your sales manager, explain hole 4 and go get one built.

Having eaten, and with a good supply of leads we are now ready to play hole 5 which is the first meeting with the prospect. Here we are going to see if we can set the bar at a realistic level so that they can become a reference-able customer.

The **5**th hole

The First Meeting is Critical

To have a great golf swing - the first lesson is critical to get the basics right. A good stance and grip, the correct swing plane and tempo, plus balance are all important if you want to go on and achieve something in golf.

It's the same for the first meeting with a new prospect. Getting off on the wrong foot will mean difficulties further down the sales cycle. Many times the first meeting, and getting the basics right, wins you the deal!

On this hole we will cover

- Why the sales manager should attend the first meeting.
- Setting the right level of expectations.
- Go or no go.
- Earning the right to solve a problem.

The sales manager should attend

How many times do you see a sale going wrong and the sales rep requests the sales manager attend a crisis meeting to sort things out? Or the deal is lost, and it's the first time anyone senior from the sales side has met the prospect?

Losing a deal early in the sales cycle could be down to a number of things like a badly qualified account, the sales rep wanting to be a superhero and doing everything him/herself, or there might have been a mismatch in functionality or personalities.

There is a point in every sale that I call "The Point of No Return". Go past that and you are dead and buried. Do something before this point and you can recover.

My call on the first meeting is that the sales manager should always attend. It means that the manager would have met some of the buyers, which will help to qualify the deal and ensure that the right expectations have been set. It will also be useful for seeing if the chemistry will be good going forward with the sales rep. But before we discuss the first meeting in more detail - a true story on why taking certain managers into a meeting might not be such a good idea!

On the tee

I was working at an IBM software house back in the 1980s. We had a sales rep (let's call him Karl) who was not all that great and the sales manager never wanted to go out on a call with him. On every account, there seemed to be some problem or other, and Dave (the sales manager) had lost confidence in Karl. This time, however, Karl had a cast iron deal and invited Dave to attend a meeting in the north, confident that they would win the deal and get his reputation back. That night Dave (who was partial to a drink or two on certain occasions) went out on a bender, did not return home, and slept the night in the office.

The next day Karl arrived bright and early to pick up his manager for the long drive ahead. He was confronted with a guy who looked a bit rough and the stink of booze could still be smelt on his breath. "Right," said Dave with a slight grimace on his face, "Let's go."

The trip was 3½ hours. When they got to within 5 miles of the prospect Karl plucked up the courage to say "Dave, I have to say that you look a bit rough. Do you think a cup of coffee would be a good idea to sharpen you up a bit?"

So off they went to the service station where they ordered two coffees. Just as Dave was about to drink his coffee, he missed his mouth and it went all down his tie and shirt.

So stinking of booze, clothes all wrinkled, bloodshot eyes, with coffee all down his shirt and tie, the sales manager arrived to close the deal. Needless to say they lasted less than 5 minutes with the prospect before they were asked to leave. I never got the lowdown, but it must have been an interesting drive back!

Just as a side note - this was a very rare occurrence as Dave was a *really* good sales manager and sales guy - but I just had to put this in the book.

Sell your weaknesses upfront

Installing an ERP system is not easy, it can take two years, takes your best people off what they are doing to become project managers, plus you have software bugs and issues. At the end of all of this it's difficult to quantify any Return On Investment.

> When I was working for JD Edwards I had a number of meetings with the main owner Ed McVaney and it often amazed me the way he would talk to customers about installing ERP systems. "You know at times you are going to get really pissed with me," he would say, "because things will go wrong. But one thing I can say is that I will be here to help you and I won't let you down when you need me."
> I liked this approach and so did the prospects.

On the tee

I had just recruited a new sales rep at JD Edwards and I wanted to attend the very first meeting with his new prospect as the project manager and a couple of user buyers were also attending.

We had a general chat and started to discuss their requirements. After a while I explained to them that our software could not do what they wanted in certain areas but we were very strong in all of the other areas. You could see the sales reps eyes getting bigger and bigger and you could read his body language. He was saying: *what the hell are you doing here? You are losing this account for me before I have started!*

I then explained to the prospect about installing ERP systems, that it's not easy, and that there would be days ahead when they would ring me up and be rather upset with me. Well, after I said that - the sales rep was thinking of all the ways he could kill me and which ones would be the most painful.

I continued however. "The difference between us and other ERP suppliers is that we are here for you *when things go wrong*, and we work the extra mile to get you out of a hole when an issue happens".

JD Edwards at this time (we were selling software for the AS/400s) had a fabulous reputation and a code of ethics that were second-to-none. We really did have great customer satisfaction.

Anyway, we all got on well and the project manager knew that buying a solution off us would mean that his job would be safe, as we were right behind him. They changed the requirements on the things we could not do, and we won the deal by 20 shots.

One of the clinchers was that our competition had started to slag off JD Edwards during the negotiations. "Did you know they can't do this, and they can't do that?" they said.

"Yes," said the project manager.

"Oh..." was the reply. "Where did you hear that from, then?"

"Directly from the company from whom we are going to buy our solution."

Every sales rep at JD Edwards UK (from then on) sold our weaknesses upfront, and that's how we got to an 80% hit rate. The last thing you need is a sales rep who can't qualify a deal, works it to the end, and then finds out that there is something the software can't do that is fundamental to the customer. You lose the deal at the 17th when you should not have even been playing the course. These sales reps are "the answer is yes! - what is the question?" brigade.

Credibility is also true for the presales team as again this adds trust. "No we can't do that," says the presales guy. "But tell me more because maybe we can handle this another way."

Selling is about selling comfort to the prospect. Letting them know that they won't be let down. This can be more important than the product or service.

On the tee

The European IT Director of Parker Hannifin, a multi-billion dollar company, gave me some great advice. "Nick," he said, "a *No* is not a problem in a sales cycle. It allows me to manage my way around a situation and provides credibility. Don't be frightened of a NO".

I sold 5 different solutions from 4 different suppliers to the company mentioned above, over a 20 year period.

Setting the right level of expectation

Many companies strive for great customer service and never achieve it for a very simple reason. The expectation during the sales cycle is set so high that customer service can never deliver it.

This is down to the sales rep overselling the product or service capabilities. Now I am not telling you to stand up and say "this is wrong, and that is wrong" - far from it. You just need to set the bar at a level you need to win the business, and this is what you need to judge at the first meeting. You might *have* to set the bar so high that it becomes a reason to no bid. In such a case, find another course you can play on. But if the prospect has realistic expectations then getting the bar right will help customer satisfaction levels down the road.

Working for a good company helps and if you find that every time you do a presentation, or have a meeting, you have to lie about things, then you owe it to yourself to join a better company, or your standards will slip.

Setting the right level of expectation will buy you credibility in the sales process and a happy customer if you can achieve a mark or two above the set level. Unhappy customers are ones that expect more than what gets delivered.

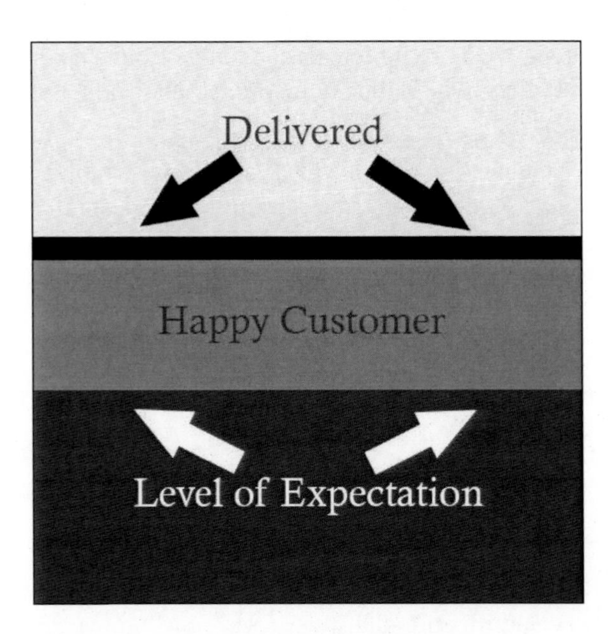

There was a time when JD Edwards was launching their open systems product just after they went public, where their standards slipped but I will be covering this, and how we coped with it, later down the course.

Go or no go

Having your sales manager at the first meeting not only shows interest in the prospect but will help to qualify an account. From the initial conversation you will be picking up on whether (or not) you will be able to sell to these people. Is there a hidden agenda(?) for example. Has a vendor's name already been pencilled in on this deal?

On the tee

Having moved into my own video marketing business, I joined a local networking company called BNI, which is one the largest and most successful business networking and referral groups in the world. I got a lead to go see a high flying businessman about a possible video ad he wanted.

I went to the office and he was busy having a meeting with another person, and kept me waiting sometime. When the meeting with the other man was over, he shook the guy's hand firmly and patted him on the back as he left the room, and then invited me to sit down. "Sit down Nick," he said. "That guy who has just left was an old friend of mine," he continued, "and he runs one of the largest video marketing companies in Buckinghamshire". It did not take me too long to get out of there. I knew to no bid.

The first meeting is where both sides are swapping information about each other. You are sizing each other up. The prospect wants to know what you can provide, whereas you want to know what the buying cycle will be, who the movers and shakers are, when they will buy, have they got the funds, who's the competition, have you a good product fit and who will sign the cheque.

This is really where hole 2 comes into play as the sales reps with high EQ will be able to get this information without coming across as too pushy. You must not be too aggressive at the first meeting as you need to *earn the right* to ask the questions above. If you don't behave 'appropriately' then you might come away with none of this valuable information.

The key is to build rapport with the prospect and plan your way to getting all the answers later down the course. Sometimes it's easy to qualify an account depending on what you have to sell.

On the tee

When JD Edwards was moving from AS/400 to open systems we only had AS/400 software to sell and the key qualification that I used was *how old was the CIO*? If they were under 35 then trying to sell AS/400 technology was a waste of time as they wanted complexity, open systems and UNIX. But if they were 55 and upwards they wanted something that worked, something that gave them a quiet couple of years before retirement.

> Finding out what is driving a decision might save you from bidding a deal you can't possibly win.

When you want something ring the week before

Do you ever get a phone call from someone you have not heard from for some time and after a few minutes of pleasantries - out comes the reason why they have called? You couldn't do me a favour could you? Or, I was wondering if you could possibly help me in this area?

There was a great technique I picked up from an agent who was based in Hong Kong. The agent was the gateway to Asia Pacific in the 1980s for IBM software houses trying to establish themselves there. We got on really well and I was able to observe what he did to get things done. If he needed something from someone he had not spoken to for a while, he would call them up and just chat about old times and ask for nothing.

Then, a week later he would call up and say "you know it was good talking to you the other day, and it just jogged my mind that you know Joe Smith from the big company down in Kowloon. I was wondering if you could introduce me to him?" No problem was the reply, totally oblivious to what his agenda was.

This is why the sales manager attending the first meeting is so important because when an account gets into trouble and the manager goes down to try to sort it out, they have already met some of the players. Management has taken the trouble to meet them the very first day they came to your office (this is like the first telephone call), so now you are more likely to receive a positive outcome at the meeting than if you had obviously been thrown in at the last minute to try to rescue the deal.

Once the first meeting is out of the way the sales manager needs to trust the sales rep to manage the sales cycle from then on.

Summary

When you are playing a round of golf, who would you rather play with: someone you know or a complete stranger? Don't miss out on the most important meeting of the round. If you are a rep – take your manager with you. If you are a manager - go down with your sales rep for the first meeting. Two heads are better than one and you should have:

- Worked out whether to bid or not.
- Found out the buying process.
- Earned the right to any subsequent meeting that might need management input from your side.
- Set the right level of expectation.

Now we are ready to play the 6th which is the first presentation to your prospects. An iron off the tee is advisable here, rather than smashing a driver out of bounds. Let's see why.

The **6**th hole

The First Presentation

Okay, the last hole mapped out what should happen at the initial meeting, but this hole is about the first *presentation*. This presentation is probably the first occasion where you meet all the people who make the decision to buy your products or services. You will probably have all of the Miller Heiman identified buyers in the room - with (maybe) the exception of the economic buyer. This is your chance to work out the informal structure of an organisation.

In golf, having a practice round is vital as it allows you to get to know the course. The more rounds you play the more familiar with the course you will become, and you should improve your chances of scoring low. The more meetings you have, the better your understanding of people's agendas should be. The first presentation is your opportunity to work out who you should 'spend time with' during the sales cycle.

On this hole we will cover

- The informal structure of an organisation.
- Why cultivating the weakest link is important.
- Talking about the prospect, not about you.
- Hidden agendas.
- Finding your coach.

Informal structure

Most sales people can work out the formal structure of an organisation. You can normally find an organisation chart or it is pretty obvious what the lines of communication are, and who reports to whom. A good CRM system will have hierarchies in place for you to enter this information. If it was appropriate to dig a little at the first meeting, you might have already found out some additional formal structural information in anticipation of the first presentation. What sales reps often miss, however, is the informal structure.

The informal structure is where someone who is not high up in the formal structure has more power than their position suggests. For example, the son of the owner working in the company at a lowly position will have a bigger influence than his formal position suggests. The external consultant, who is a personal friend to the CEO, needs to be respected. An up and coming employee who is being fast tracked to take over from someone more senior, and the person who is after his boss's job, are all people that need to be identified and respected.

On the tee

We were presenting JD Edwards to a privately held UK company. At the first meeting there was the chairman, CFO, CEO, and CIO, as well as technical and economic buyers.

The chairman sat down and everyone then took their seats. Right next to the chairman a very attractive lady CIO sat down, whilst the CFO was on the left. As I observed the rest of the team taking their places the informal structure started to take shape. The informal *hierarchy of importance* literally flowed from the head of the table down. Let's face it, a person who has just joined the company as an IT programmer would not pop himself down next to the chairman.

> A little historical note. The term "right hand man" comes from the court of a King. The King would place his top adviser to his right hand side. It was the most important place to sit.

Anyway as the meeting progressed it was clear that the CIO was not as technical as she should have been to hold down her job. My radar was on the blink and I needed to find out more.

We had managed to find our coach, who was the chief accountant, at our first meeting. He had heard of JD Edwards and wanted us for our financial software. It was not long before we found out that the chairman was having a 'private relationship' with the CIO, and she had recently been promoted from IT manager. In other words - get her vote and you have the chairman's vote.

As the meeting went on you could easily spot the movers and shakers, the key decision makers and the ones that no one paid any attention to. The people that asked the most questions are not necessarily the main decision makers. Don't forget the internal politics within any prospect's company. People who ask questions could be showing off in front of their boss, or trying to score points. What you are looking for are the Empathy Selling Politicians (P_s) in the organisation; these are the best people to cultivate as they drive their own ideas through.

Politicians will never want to look stupid in the eyes of their subordinates so only a few might ask questions, especially when they are of a technical nature, at the first meeting.

So we had spotted most of the key personnel. But now, we did something else, and I am going to suggest something that you won't find in any sales training.

Cultivate the Weakest Link

For the sake of simplicity, and for our UK audience, I am going to call the Weakest Link a "W". Now rule number one is that a "W" does not know they are a "W". This is so important that I am going to highlight it.

> The Weakest Link *does not* know they are the Weakest Link.

For a "W" it's a continuing surprise that no one listens to them, or takes up any of their ideas, or that they are always getting passed over for promotion. Not realising they are a "W" is why they are a "W".

Most sales reps will gravitate towards the key decision makers as they are the ones who make the decisions and who have the politician's characteristic of wanting their own way (as above).

However, very few sales reps will cultivate the "W" as they are seen to be unimportant, with no value in a sale. Wrong! The "W" *is* part of the team; he or she attends every meeting, they are party to most of the decisions, and most importantly they will tell you what is going on as, remember, they are a "W".

The movers and shakers will not look to give anything away to the supplier as they want the best deal at the end, and want to give the impression that it is still a competitive deal right down to the wire. The "W" will tell you everything if you cultivate them successfully.

On the tee

We were selling to a large retail organisation. At the presentation was a guy who had been with the company for years and was in charge of the general ledger. He sat on his own at the end of the table and no one took much notice of him. He clearly was the "W" in the team.

I decided to cultivate him, and we went down to see him where he showed us how all the journals were processed and what the old system did. He was so excited that we were giving him the time of day. "You know no one has ever asked me what I do, or spent this amount of time with me. I really like your product and would love to have it in here." We found out everything that was going on from that point onwards, and won this deal very easily.

There is always a "W" in every organization

Just a side story here. At one of the companies I was at, we were moving from a consulting based to a product based business model, and we had a number of people who were not fitting in. We had recruited a good friend of mine to run support and it was in his department that we had the issues. So we bit the bullet and let some people go.

A week later we went to the US for a meeting. We were collected from the airport by the American CEO and we started discussing what had happened, and what the strategy was going to be. All of a sudden my friend said: "Isn't it good that we have no Ws left in the company anymore," and we all turned around to him and just laughed and said, a "W" does not know he is a "W". The penny dropped and he joined in, and the whole car was in fits of laughter. Rule number two. It's always good to be able to identify a "W" in your company because if you can't, it may be that the "W" is you!

It's all about them

The first presentation is so important. Not only are you going to learn so much about your prospect's informal structure, internal politics and who to cultivate, but by using everything you have learnt from the initial meeting on hole 4, it will enable you to present a solution that will solve their business issues. In turn, if your competition is presenting all about themselves, it will differentiate you from day one. Let me explain.

JD Edwards was late, in comparison to other US software houses, to set up in Europe. With our manufacturing software we were starting to come up against the market leader in the IBM AS/400 market place.

We had just recruited a few of their people and I asked them how they went about presenting the company at the first demo.

"Oh," said the sales rep, "we had all these PowerPoint slides that we went through, telling them just how good we were. We are the biggest and the best in the world and we have done this, and we have done that."

So basically they were telling their prospects that you must be mad if you don't buy from us. When you are the biggest – you are probably doing something right. And if you underscore that point (we are the biggest because we are the best), it is a strong sell.

So when we had our first competitive deal against them we were on the back foot. How on earth are we going to win against this?

I decided that we were going to tailor our first meeting / demonstration to what the prospect needed. We went down and found out what the issues were. We got hold of a product catalogue and set up some real products. When we started the demo we did not say anything about our company. We focused on *their* requirements and their problems - getting feedback along the way that we were on the right track.

"One of the issues you have is that you need to be able to configure a product on the fly; is that correct?" we asked.

"Yes," was the reply, and a big discussion broke out as to why they could not do it.

We then showed them what we had built and the manufacturing director got up and started to use the software (obviously a kinaesthetic person). The chemistry was just electric with this prospect and they left the office as if they were long lost friends. We were winning the deal and we kept focusing on solving their issues. They could not wait to get the software installed.

The sale became a no contest from then on but we never got complacent. Later, when we had a debriefing (after we won) they told us that the competitor just could not show them anything real, everything was PowerPoint, and how they were the biggest and the best ERP solution for the AS/400 platform. But they never saw any software, let alone software with their data. One of the things I did was to ban the 'company pitch' which really focused the minds of the sales team. From then on, they had to start off any presentation on the prospect's issues.

This was another competitor against whom we had an 80% hit rate.

Show! Don't just tell!

First meeting blues

Now this is something I would not recommend trying as a sales tactic, but I want to pass on this true story. At one particular first meeting, we were just starting the product demonstration and there was this individual who kept on asking silly questions. Our presales guy was not the best person to suffer fools and I could see he was getting more and more flustered with the questions that kept coming his way.

Eventually he cracked and just blurted out that these questions were really dumb and they had no relevance to their solution. Ouch! Well you could have heard a pin drop.

People hated the presales guy, and by association they now hated my sales guy and me. We were getting painted with the same brush, and the mood in the room went from grim to full on terrible.

We said our au revoirs and hurriedly went into a meeting room to see what we were going to do next. Clearly we were now in a losing position. To be fair, the presales guy put up his hand up and apologised to us right away. The only way forward was for him to write a formal letter of apology to the questioner, which he did, and ask for a meeting. He said that it was clear that he had not understood the questions that had been asked at the meeting, and would like to get some first-hand experience of the issues.

We got the meeting and he apologised formally again, shook hands, and listened to everything his bête noir said. The next meeting was great. We were loved again and the presales guy had gone the extra mile to make sure all the requirements were covered. The rest of the team loved us again, and we won the deal.

> Sometimes, if you get off to a really bad start, look to manufacture an opportunity to get closer to your prospect.

Hidden agendas

The first meeting is also very important to see if there are any hidden agendas bubbling away, or whether there are particular people who will influence this deal further down the course. At coffee breaks it's vitally important to enter into small talk. Make sure that the folks on your side of the room are all asking the same type of questions to whomever they talk with.

- How long have you worked at this company?
- Where did you used to work before here?
- What systems did you have then?
- Were you happy with those systems, and if not - what were the problems?
- Does your company use consultants, and if so, who?

You are looking for biases that might come out later. Also add some social chat:

- What do you get up to when you have some spare time?
- What's your passion?
- What is your favourite football team?

LinkedIn is a great tool to find out a lot of this information and people are not to know that you have already done your research on them beforehand. Small talk is essential to build rapport so that more probing questions can be asked later when "you have earned the right" to ask them.

Don't just focus on business; you need to get to know the person and take a genuine interest in them. Small talk is an art and vital in sales. These simple questions will lead to vital clues into the hidden agendas that people might have.

Finding out if there are any third party consultants involved is important, especially if they get involved later on in the sale. If they are attending, you need to know where their expertise lies. If, for example, you have a third party consultant that knows your competition – this should be a red flag as it might mean they want the implementation later (after the deal has been signed).

Remember all these conversations need to be natural and this is where people with high EQ will come into their own. If it's not appropriate to ask then don't, and you will have to find out this information another way; once you have cultivated your coach, for example.

The coach

Okay, so you have recognised who the "W" is but now it's time to find out who your coach is. Most times the coach finds you. If, for example, someone already knows about your company and wants you to win - they will gravitate to the sales rep and engage in conversation, and information will flow freely. Empathy Selling Movers (Ms) as we discovered on hole 2, will want to talk and might appear to be the type of people to cultivate, which you have to cover anyway, but they might not be a great coach as they will be friendly to your competition as well as you.

It's the more thoughtful person who is high in the organisational chart, or who has a strong influence in the informal structure that you need to look out for. If you have not identified someone by the 6th hole then you will need to think long and hard about playing the 7th. Don't forget the rule "no coach no deal".

Summary

Everyone is important in an evaluation team and sometimes the less obvious person can hold the key to the deal. Being observant and watching people's behaviour is essential in understanding how they rank in the informal structure of an organisation. In turn, presenting a solution to a problem is better than talking about your own company. Shooting 64 is better than saying what you might do.

By now you will have cultivated the "W" and identified your coach. You have now had the chance to work out the main players and searched for any hidden agendas that might stop this deal from happening. We are now ready to move on to the 7th hole where we are going to have a critical review of this account and plan our way to success.

The **7** th hole

How are we Doing?

You've had your initial meeting, finished the first demo, and things are looking good. It's now time to have a critical review of the account. In any truthful review you will come out feeling depressed and unsure because you will have more questions than answers, more doubts than certainties. This is normal.

It's like getting off to a good start with a few birdies and a par and then you're left wondering *when* it is all going to go wrong, and you start to get worried and fret about the rest of the round.

On this hole we will cover

- When should you do a review?
- What you should cover.
- Bid or no bid; devise your plan of attack.

When should you do a sales review?

Reviews should be done with your sales manager at any time, and should not be confined to sales meetings, although the odd review will also be of interest to other members of the team especially if they can learn from the review process.

Reviews are normally called for when the sales rep starts to feel uncomfortable about the deal and wants to get a second opinion on it. The manager should use the review as an audit on the sales rep to check that they are on the right path. As a manager if you have a rep that is closing 80% of his business you don't need to worry too much unless they ask for your help. But if you have a rep that is struggling then you might need to do reviews more regularly.

Some reviews could be over an informal coffee or drink after work, just bouncing ideas and issues off your managers or other sales reps. Other reviews, if you do them properly, can take a good morning to complete. From the review you will come up with an action plan but these plans need to be flexible and you need to constantly monitor how things are going all of the time. Great sales reps can do a review in their head in real time but even the very best will come out of a detailed review meeting with their manager with some actions that they had not thought of.

Miller Heiman has a review process called the blue sheet and if you follow their process you won't miss much. Nonetheless, here are key concepts I cover when I conduct a review.

Organizational structure

When I do a review, I want to know the structure of the prospect's company and the formal and informal organizational hierarchies - as this fast-tracks me on where we stand with any account.

1. I find out if the sales rep knows this information which will give me confidence.
2. It gives me a feel for all the players in the deal.

Selling to a US multinational, for example, is a nightmare. You will often find the UK CEO saying that he *has* the authority to buy, only to find out that he does not, or that he is about to be fired and therefore has no buying power. This is a red flag which gets highlighted on the CRM system. A red flag is a weakness in the bid, something that is a problem and needs looking into.

Also when selling to a division of a domestic multinational it's a big mistake to think that because one division of a multinational company has your solution - you then have a better chance of selling into a sister company. Quite the opposite.

On the tee

We were selling to a division of a multinational biscuit company that already had our solution in two divisions. I was trying to sell to a third division, but we lost and I just could not understand why. Later I found out that there was a big rift between this division and the others, and they held an attitude that they wanted to do the total opposite of what the group wanted or what other divisions did. We missed this vital information in the sales campaign as we were overconfident of winning this deal because of our past record.

So, by looking into a prospect's corporate structure you are trying to find out who can and cannot make decisions, and looking to find out where the influence really lies. I differentiate multinational companies into:

1. Single focused multinational companies like GlaxoSmithKline which tend to have HQ driven decisions. GlaxoSmithKline are into pharmaceuticals. That's their main business and they need common processes worldwide.
2. Diverse multinationals which have a number of different types of organizations reporting to corporate headquarters. Management at HQ will buy and sell these companies all the time and these companies will have more autonomy on what they purchase. The need for common practices across these companies is not required.

Once you get a feel for the company's structure you now need to move onto the interesting part: people. I know this is an obvious statement but never forget that it is people who make a buying decision not the company. GlaxoSmithKline does not buy anything, but Fred Smith et al. (who work for GlaxoSmithKline) do. All of these people will have their own personal agendas, fears and ego. This next section is where a sales rep with high EQ comes into their own.

Important people

So from the first meeting and first demo you should now be building up a list of key individuals. The buyers will be the coach, user buyers, technical buyers, anti coach and economic buyer. You will need to know their roles, degree of importance, and what mode are they in. Mode is an interesting concept that can be split into four. Miller Heiman defines mode as:

- *Growth mode:* the company is not coping with increased business using their current systems or service, and is putting pressure on the buyer to do something about it. The probability of getting a deal is high.
- *Troubled mode:* expected results are not being achieved and buying your product or service would solve the problem. Again the chances of getting a deal here are high.
- *Even keel mode:* the buyer does not feel that he has to do anything and feels as though they are coping okay and delivering the expected results for the company. This buyer would be wary of any change and would not want to rock the boat with any new system or service.
- *Overconfident mode:* the buyer can't see any problems and there is absolutely no need for your products or services, and the chances of getting a sale here are zero.

A number of deals are lost to a "*do nothing decision*" or "*just having a look at the market*" and it is by working out the mode of the buyers that will really determine whether there is a real drive to do something

Part of the sale review would be to work out a plan focused on how you can get someone from even keel to trouble or growth mode. Point out that there is new legislation coming that will mean that what they do today can't be done with the systems they currently have. Open their minds into how installing a new system will help their career path. Someone who is overconfident and not open to any change will be a problem and you need to sell around them unless they are the key decision maker (which could lead you straight off the course into the 19th). If they can't see a need for change then you are probably on the wrong golf course! Another reason for change is *their* competition… are they doing better than your target prospect? Do they have cunning plans that are changing the game? Maybe they already have your software and that's why they are more nimble and can react to market demands more quickly.

Degree of influence

As the title suggests – this is all about how much influence individuals hold. This is quite simple and you can put a grading system in place.

1. *High trump*: this person is so important that he or she can change anything at any time.
2. *High*: has a major say in what will happen.
3. *Medium*: has a mid-level say in what will happen.
4. *Low*: has little impact on the process.
5. *Seemingly Irrelevant*: but could be important to helping you in the sale. As we saw on hole 6, they could be a "W" and need a friend. Someone who is irrelevant from their company point of view, if cultivated correctly, could move you up the food chain as they will supply you with good information.

Remember the informal hierarchy when you work this out as the son of the owner might be low in the formal structure but would still be classified as high influence.

What's in it for them?

This is so important. Can you put down next to the buyer's name what *they* would get out of buying your solution? How it would change their lives? The more the better. If you are scratching your head trying to think of something, then you are in trouble. Again this could lead you to exit the course.

I can remember coming up with a great win for the user buyer: "you can do your job so much quicker with our software - you will have more spare time". This sounded like a compelling reason to buy. However, it can also be a problem. Let me explain.

On the tee

When I was running the sales at The GL Company – we had a unique product that enabled people to produce reports and information in a fraction of the time compared to traditional spreadsheets and Business Intelligence tools. At one prospect's business, there was an individual who spent three days a week putting data into a spreadsheet and then building complex macros that only he knew - to get a set of accounts together. The rest of the week he would spend analysing where these numbers had come from within the ERP system.

We came along and in 2 hours eliminated three days of his time. Now, do you put this down as a selling point to this particular individual? *Absolutely not* because how was he going to justify having a job at this company? He was indispensable as no-one knew the analysis formulae.

So to get this deal we needed to go higher up the organizational chain and find out what this guy would be doing with his time once our system went in. We were then able to calm him down so that he could see how he would spend most of his time interpreting the information rather than assembling it.

An (almost) unbelievable true story

We managed to get this same software into a really large multinational PLC and quickly discovered some really big variances on their consolidated trial balance. We found 20% of the issue right away and I went back to the office really excited.

The next day I could not get hold of the guy in the IT department. I called the financial accountant, then one down from the CFO, then the internal audit guy - but nothing. It was like I had the plague. They never bought from us, they never spoke to us again. There was too much at stake in this company as we had found something wrong with the in-house built consolidated reporting system.

It was in no-one's interest to have our software apart from the shareholders who were not making the decision.

> Sometimes a positive win from your perspective could end up being a negative one from the buyer's point of view.

What's their rating?

Can you put a value next to each buyer from +5 to -5? Can you quantify your level of support? Here is a list of marks.

+5 Really want you
+4 Strongly on board
+3 Onboard
+2 Interested
+1 Will go along

-1 Won't rock the boat
-2 Uninterested
-3 Luke warm on you
-4 Favours the competition
-5 The anti-coach

How much time have you spent with each buyer?

A simple high, medium and low grade will cover this. Spending time with the prospect is the key to winning the deal. The more meetings you have, the less the competition can have. If you are not getting access to buyers then you are in trouble as they are spending their time with another supplier.

Also if they are willing to give you this time then this is a good indication of the progress you are making.

For me the people aspect is the most important part of an account review. As I said before (but I will repeat it) it is people not companies that make decisions. It sounds obvious but it all comes back to having EQ and being able to extract feedback from these buyers into knowing exactly how you are doing, without asking them directly. You know when you have done a good demo? So *don't ask* how it went at the end of it! What are they going to say? "Yes it went well, thank you", even if it went badly.

Account reviews can get very tiresome so I think it's time for a story. It has all happened to us, the *demo from hell* when everything goes wrong. When it does, sometimes it really is better to say nothing at all at the end.

On the tee

Why saying nothing might just be a good idea… the demo from hell, and how not to run a demonstration.

I was in charge of selling and marketing AMIS (Advanced Management Information System) back in 1987. AMIS was our new BI system for the AS/400, and it was a separate division from the main core financial and distribution system. I had managed to work a deal with the other sales teams. If they ran into major competition and needed an edge in a sale they would work with me. I would get paid on my deal and the other division would get paid on all the other products they sold.

We had a really complex account where there was a need for the software to cater for seven different countries, and where foreign currency capabilities were a big requirement. The sales manager for the other division decided to go with the old software as he thought it could handle the requirements.

The day of the demo arrived and I was in one of the offices working on a new release for AMIS. Part of the new release required me to convert my existing demo files. Thinking that I had a clear day ahead of me I started the conversion. This was going to be a big mistake.

We were pitching to the prospect, and the demo was to a room full of people from different nationalities. We kicked off with our CEO introducing everyone in our company and because he was multi-lingual, he thought he should do this in a number of languages. This did not go down well at all, and after 5 minutes he was stopped by the prospect's project manager who asked him to speak in English.

Then we got into the demo and our sales rep, Paul was leading the charge. It was soon clear that he was in big trouble as they needed multi-currency for the AP and AR modules, but a dual currency base GL, which the old product could not do.

Rich (the sales manager) entered my office "Nick. Can you come downstairs and help us out," he asked. "Can you come to the demo room and show them AMIS? We need a dual currency GL."

I had not tested the conversion but I hurried into the demo room and started to explain the solution. I then went to the software and began demonstrating how you put through a journal. When I hit the <enter> key the software blew up with error messages everywhere.

Unperturbed, I pushed on. "So," I said, "let's pretend that we have entered a journal, and we wish to inquire on it." I went to the inquiry screen where I knew we had some data but this option blew up as well. Five more options blew up as I tried to demonstrate the software, the conversion had corrupted all my data and I was dying up there.

I was dying onstage – and all I could think was: this is Rich's fault. He should have got me involved in this deal from the beginning then I would not have converted the files.

My only course of action was to simply make my excuses, walk out, and hand everything back to Rich. So Rich wheeled Paul back into the demo and he reverted back to the old software and some serious spin which got the prospects to the lunch break.

In the afternoon, the prospect was going to see AP in action. The demo was to be run by another presales person called Dave, but Rich was getting worried as Dave appeared not to be in the office. The demo was about to restart… no sign of Dave.

So with no Dave, Paul stepped up to the plate. He had a quiet word in Rich's ear. "I will finish off this demonstration."

Paul went back into the demo room. There were 14 people from the prospect's company, and one of him. No-one from our company wanted to go anywhere near this demo now.

Rich and I watched the presentation from a glass window that overlooked the conference room. Paul was out of his depth but to his lasting credit he just kept on and answered questions the best he could, although he would not have known in detail what he was talking about.

Rich turned to me. "Nick we have lost this deal. What are we going to do?"

"Just let it pan out Rich," I advised. "You can't do anything now, but don't say anything about the demo now."

Rich was so devastated that when everyone on the prospect's side started to leave he just began to apologize to everyone. Eventually he stopped our coach. "I am so sorry," said Rich. "This was the worst demo I have ever given. Please forgive me."

"Yes. I thought it was not very good, Rich. We will be in touch."

Thought? I wondered if Rich had said nothing whether we might have got away with it!

Needless to say this deal was lost and we handed our competition an early Christmas present.

Sometimes, *saying nothing* is the best call.

Okay, back to the account review as this was an easy account to work out.

Do they have a business case?

For any company to spend millions of dollars on a new project or system there must have been a business case written, reviewed by the board, and signed off. What you need to ascertain is, what are the business benefits that the company is going to achieve once they have purchased the service or system? This can then be used as a focus in future demonstrations where you can reinforce the business benefits and how they relate to your solution. If this is not forthcoming or there is no business case written, then this is a red flag as the project could simply be an information gathering exercise used to compile a business case, with no guarantee that anything will get approval.

If this is the case you then need to qualify if you are willing to do further work to help the prospect build the business case around your solution. You can probably add six months to a year on the sales cycle if this is the case. Also the biggest competitor to you on this account is "Do Nothing" which is a competitor that you can't do much about, and which unfortunately pops up all too frequently.

On the tee

We received an Invitation To Tender (ITT) which after consideration really appeared to be something we did not want to bid on. It looked like it had come straight out of the back of a training manual on how to put an ITT together and covered everything you can think of. Anyway we telephoned the prospect and told them that we did not think we had a good fit but they insisted on coming in to see us.

When they arrived they levelled with us and said that there was no budget but they really needed some help in putting an ITT and business case together. We got on like a house on fire and we managed to change a number of their requirements that, funnily enough, our product was really good at.

Months later we received the new ITT which had been approved by the board and we could tick a 'yes' against every question, as the ITT had been written by us.

> If there is no business case written then help the prospect. Write one.

Compelling event

A compelling event is a reason why a company needs to make a decision. The year 2000, when companies believed that their ERP software was going to fail because they could not enter 4 characters in the date field, drove a lot of software sales. When Euro currency coins and banknotes entered circulation on 1 January 2002 this was another good reason to buy new equipment and software.

Companies that have been sold off from the parent company and are being thrown off the parent company's computer systems by a certain date is also a great compelling event as these companies have to buy 'something'.

You need to find out what the compelling event is for any account and if you can't find one then you need to create an event. Price and the availability of your company's staff to start a project are compelling events that you can control but if there is no real driving event then this deal could drag on, and again you need to consider whether or not it is worth bidding.

Build your sales plan

Okay, so you have your account review, and out of this you have two options, *no bid* where you go straight to the 19th (although it might be a bit too early to play this card; we will be discussing this further down the course) or *bid*. If you are bidding then you need a plan on what you are going to do, who is going to do it, and when.

You will need to come up with strategies. Strategies like:

- Getting access to the CEO. Or the most senior exec that is appropriate to the size of the deal.
- Spending more time with the production director - understanding his needs and showing him the win that will be gained from using your solution.
- Getting the coach fully into this deal so that he is committed for you to win.
- How to ensure each buyer sees a win from taking your solution, and how to demonstrate this win to them.

The list is endless but only you can work this out.

Summary

The 7th hole is too early in the round to know exactly what your chances are of winning this deal but you can certainly tell if you are losing. Account reviews should be happening in the sales rep's mind all the time because things can change on a daily basis.

Just because you have a review one week and everything looks okay today does not mean this will continue to be the case in a week's time.

Now if you have decided that you are going to go for this account as you have identified all the key buyers and the company has a compelling event - you need to go for it 100%. We are ready to play the 8th which is committing to this round and giving it your very best shot. Failure is not an option.

The 8th hole

Commit to the Deal, Multi-Level Selling

Failure is not an option. Never bid a deal where you are not going for it 100%. If you play half-heartedly during a round, you will never score to the best of your ability.

What you will learn on this hole

- 100% or nothing.
- Multi-Level Selling.
- Large Account Engagement rule.
- Good Cop, Bad Cop.

100% or nothing

You have just finished the 7th hole (the account review) and you now need to work out whether or not you can win this account. Are there any hidden agendas? Could a third party sink your bid? Is there a budget? Do you have a coach? Is there a compelling event?

By now you should have enough information to determine whether you want to go for the sale, or not. You should have a sales strategy in mind so that if it's a go, you need to commit totally, and utilize all the tips coming up in the holes ahead.

> Never bid a deal half-heartedly as you will almost certainly lose.

This is a typical problem with certain companies that you may work for - management would rather *see* a sales rep working on a deal even though the chances of winning are slim, instead of the sales rep doing nothing.

Looking busy and losing is a waste of your time and your company's resources, winning is the only acceptable outcome of a sales cycle (or walking off the course early to find another course you can play). Coming second gets you nothing.

My philosophy was that if you needed to hit $2m in sales at an average deal size of $500k then that could be 4 or 5 deals, or sometimes it could be just *one*. You have a year to do it in, and the sales cycle is between 4 and 6 months, so why bid on 12 deals that take up pre-sales resources and management time when you can bid on 6 and hit your number?

Having too many deals means that you can't possibly give all of them the attention they need. If you chase 2 rabbits - both will escape.

I would rather a sales rep be on a real golf course with a prospect or customer instead of bidding bad business as they will not waste my time and company resources. Now I don't really mean that they should be on the golf course every day but hopefully you get my point. Sales reps can always find something useful to do but should avoid taking up resources unless they are going to win some business.

Now that you have whittled down your pipeline, you really need to roll out the plan you derived from hole 7. But there are some other key areas to cover over and above the Miller Heiman blue sheet if you are going to give this sale total commitment.

Multi-Level Selling

In a complex sale there will be many people involved in the process from both the prospect and vendor ends. You need to get your team lined up with theirs and if you are struggling to get access to C level executives then this is a red flag and needs to be managed. Having a good coach is a way to help you get access to C level executives.

> Multi-Level Selling requires everyone at every level of the buying team to be covered by your team. Even saying 'yes' at the very top will not guarantee your deal if you have not sold lower down.

On the tee

The CFO of one of our customers (who had the financial suite installed at head office) was very keen to install our new distribution suite. I went to the head office and enjoyed a great meeting with two board members; if it had been their choice I would have walked out with the order there and then. They informed me that we had come in a bit late in the deal as there had been an on-going evaluation but we just needed to convince the production team that our solution was acceptable to them. We were asked to do a demonstration and off we went - totally confident that this was just a delay in the deal as we had such strong support from the board.

Needless to say we were greeted by the production team with hostility as they had already chosen their solution and were upset that HQ were getting involved. But with the support of the board surely these people would change their minds and want our solution?

Internal politics on the prospect's side is something that is easy to miss. The sale (or should I say loss of this sale) taught me a big lesson.

After we had shown our software the production team came across as very 'unsympathetic' to our solution. They simply did not want to change their decision and I hurriedly called up the CFO and explained the situation. I explained that middle management wanted a competitive product and we had been brought in too late in the day to change their minds. I cut to the chase - as you are their boss surely you can just overrule them?

The answer was *no* for a very good reason. "C" people don't do, and in many cases can't do, middle management roles, yet they totally rely on them. This is why companies employ middle management in the first place. There was no way that the CFO could go over their heads; it was just like telling them that he had no trust in what they do.

"Nick, I just can't do this. I am going to have to go along with the management team's decision on this - even though I want your solution."

So we had won the board but lost middle management and in most cases it is more important to get the vote of middle management, as these are the very people that are going to use the solution and have to live with it every day.

Large account engagement rules

If you are dealing with a multinational company then Multi-Level Selling can become very complex but still needs to be done. You could be selling to a local division, for example, and this is fine if you are sure that the division can make a purchasing decision but I would really worry if the HQ is in another country. As we discovered on hole 7, so many times you are told by the local CEO that they can make a decision only to find out they cannot.

The very best policy is to contact HQ and cover the key buyers rather than burying your head in the sand and hoping it will sort itself out. The real question here is *who is going to make the call to the HQ?*

I really don't think that many companies have a good multinational engagement policy but if you can get this right you will win many more deals. At JD Edwards we had a number of multinational plans over the 10 years I was there; in fact we had as many plans as we had different CEOs which were 5 in total over this period of time. They all had different ideas on how to make people work together across territories. The best one was when we all *double bubbled*, that's when everyone gets paid on the same deal regardless of influence. Although this affects the gross margin it drives more business in the short term. Long term, however, double bubbling is commercial suicide as the cost is far too high.

At the time we were losing multinational deals to the market leader but with this plan in place we had a number of surprising wins against them.

On the tee

We were selling to a very large pharmaceutical company that traditionally had bought from our main competitor. The deal was going into three continents and I was running the European part of the deal.

We were all up for this sale and we had the US sales team leading the charge with everyone else supporting. We did a number of demos and we soon started to build relationships with our target prospect. The message that we were getting from our prospect was that no one from the competition was doing any demonstrations let alone meeting with them.

We won this account at a canter and we got all the votes from the regions. The US HQ was forced to make a decision in our favour even though they preferred the market leader because of the wave of support for us from around the world. This taught me the importance of getting as many people as you can involved in a deal - but this does have to be managed. A great large-account plan will do this for you and I have enclosed one that I wrote for The GL Company that protects margins and incentivizes sales reps to work together. See Appendix B.

In due course, we hired a few of our competitor's employees and they told me that they did not have a multinational plan as the HQ sales reps got all the commission and there was no reason for anyone in the territories to become involved. This explained the lack of activity outside the US which led to our rival's loss of the sale.

Good cop, bad cop

Sometimes an unpopular call needs to be made, so by having two people covering one buyer, you can sacrifice one person to make the call. Here a *Good Cop Bad Cop* approach is required.

Selling is not charity and if you don't sell you won't last long in the job. There are many times when you will need to exert pressure on a prospect to close the deal. If the prospect has a compelling event then great - they need to do something. But as discussed earlier in chapter 7, if they don't, you need to make one up.

If your 'year end' does not line up with your prospect's compelling event then you need to make one up. Normally this is price, or it could be availability of staff to start a project.

I have typically had great relationships with my prospects but there is always a time in the sales cycle that you need to be very firm. But how do you do this without breaking the relationship?

This is the time you need a good cop and a bad cop because someone needs to tell the prospect that if they go past a certain date - the cost of taking your solution is going to rise. Many a time I have asked a sales rep to be firm on a close. Afterwards I would get a phone call from the prospect complaining about my rep. I can then have a frank conversation and really get out of the prospect whether the deal can be closed, or if they genuinely have the authority that they say they have. Sometimes I needed to be the bad cop.

On the tee

We were selling to a division of a $10bn US multinational company and I had previously had a meeting with the CEO of one of the divisions prior to their purchase of our software in the UK. They now wanted to negotiate a worldwide licence and the CEO asked if I would come in to meet his number two whom I had not met.

I went to their office and I was bang on time. I was kept waiting for nearly an hour at reception and all I could see was this rolling demo (on a TV screen) of how they were the largest company in the world at what they did, and how they had offices everywhere.

The secretary eventually came down and asked me to follow her. I was thinking… this is going to be a big deal.

When I went into the office there were two guys. The first I knew. The second was the number two. Both were looking glum and weren't particularly keen to exchange pleasantries. The number two was a raging Empathy Selling Politician. He was the one who had kept me waiting an hour and was straight down to business.

"Nick we want to buy a worldwide licence. What's your price?"

"Well this is a difficult question. How many sites are you looking at? Where are they located? What business divisions are we talking about?" I asked.

It was not long before the number two offered his value for the software. "We are prepared to pay 100k."

"Is that in Sterling or US dollars?" I asked (not that this was going to be relevant).

"Dollars," was the reply.

Now $100,000 would be around 20 power users for our software. So, for a worldwide deal, and without knowing exactly how many users, countries and divisions the software would be implemented in, this was clearly not going to fly.

After a number of attempts on why I could not do this $100k deal I said to the two guys: "We really are not getting very far here, are we?"

This was met with silence.

"I am sorry but I just can't help you," I said. "We are so far apart that we can't do a deal."

Again there was a big pause. I offered my hand, said my goodbyes, and left.

No sooner had I got to my car than I got a frantic call from Joe, the sales rep. "Nick I have had a call from my contact who said that you have been really rude and that this was the worst meeting the number two had ever been in."

I explained the situation and we decided that my sales rep would now become the sales director (main point of contact) and I would be the big bad wolf in the background. Even to this day I found that meeting to be one of the most bizarre that I have ever attended, and I put this down to internal politics at their end. They were having trouble rolling out JD Edwards and they needed our software but they had no budget to buy it, so they just tried to bully me into giving them the software.

Joe did a great job in managing them and over the years we managed to close over $500,000 of software just from the one division with four more to go. The company was still held in high esteem by the customer. It was just that Nick Gomersall who was the big bad (and rude) guy.

More of this when we come to hole 17: contract negotiations.

Lining up your management team

If you are bidding on a significant deal then you will want to get the top management from your side involved. In fact they will probably insist that they have some involvement. You need to line them up with their equivalents from the prospect's side. Now this is a very tricky time as you have to brief your boss and his boss on what to say. In effect the sales rep becomes the boss and the other guys are now working for you.

There is one big problem here - a number of times the person at the very top might not be great in front of a prospect, what to do?

On the tee

I am sure Ed McVaney (the owner of JD Edwards at the time) won't mind me telling this story. Ed was working with me in the early days of setting up JD Edwards in the UK and Europe. Ed wanted to get close to the localisation issues that make it hard to sell software in Europe. Italy had strange VAT (IVA) issues, France had legal requirements called the

Plan Contable, and they had a tax deduction on the payroll for the postman if they have to ride their bicycle up a mountain to deliver a letter to a monastery, or something like that. You get the point.

Now the first time I got Ed involved in a deal we were on the back foot and clearly (as new kids on the block) we were in a losing position. In we went and Ed met the CEO of my prospect. Ed was great, he sold credibility and told the CEO what the plans were for the UK *and* Europe, which were of interest to him as they were a number of sites outside of the UK. He turned the deal around and we won the account.

The next time we used Ed we were winning an account. This meeting was not so good as we got into detail on 'chart of account design' for the general ledger and there was a disagreement between Ed and the CEO. Needless to say Ed turned the deal round again, this time from a winning position to a losing one.

We had a good chat about it and managed to see the funny side of this and we christened Ed from then on "The Turnaround Kid" so next time Ed wanted to come along to meet a prospect he would firstly say: "Are you winning or losing?" Needless to say, Ed only came on losing deals from then on.

> When you involve higher management make sure that they are properly briefed on all the issues, and what their objective(s) in meeting the prospect should be.

Summary

Okay, let's take stock. We are off and running and now have a sales plan in place. We have identified the people from our end that need to double up with the prospect's formal and informal organisational structure.

Spending time with your prospects is key, the more time you spend the less your competition has with them. The more time you spend with them, the more likely you are to win.

> No one spends significant time with people they don't want to buy from.

As the great Gary Player said: "The harder you work, the luckier you get." Let's play the 9th and see how you can ensure that by always 'having a valid purchasing reason to discuss things' - you will always get face time.

The **9** th hole

Last One through the Door

The more meetings you have with a prospect - the better your chances of closing the deal. If you want to improve your game you need to spend time on the range.

On this hole we will cover

- No talk, no deal.
- Too much information leads to lack of contact.
- Will they go down the pub?
- Sales 2.0: dangerous or useful?

If you are not talking to your prospects you are not winning

You have just had a great presentation and everything went well. You all shook hands and as your prospect leaves the building you are already banking your commission cheque in your head. But a week later you get a frantic call from your coach to say that all is not well, you are now in second place and you need to do something. So how did that happen?

If possible always go last

Constant communication is essential in winning a deal and one of the best ways to ensure that you are talking to your prospect last is by 'going last' in any presentation. People's memories are short, and by going last you have the final opportunity to sell. In turn, prospects can also get confused when bombarded with lots of information from different sales people, so it's also an opportunity to clarify what your business proposition is.

I can remember one particular prospect who had looked at 5 vendors in the final month and they were so confused as to *who could do what* that when it came to the final presentation they had invented a solution that comprised all 5 vendors!

Going last enabled us to refocus this prospect's point of view. We went through the benefits of our solution which remained fresh in their minds for the final meeting (the next day) when the decision on who would be the last two on the shortlist was to be made. Needless to say we were on the list.

Going last also allows the prospect to raise all the issues your competitors might have planted in their minds about the problems they will have with your solution. Solving these issues will give them the reassurance they need to take you forward to the final two.

It's a self-evident statement but it's vital to have as much face time as realistically possible and this is why I have dedicated a hole to this point. This is why I drew the distinction between sales and lead generation (marketing) on hole 4; when you are really doing a good job of selling you simply don't have the time to generate leads as well.

If you can't go last then you really need to arrange a meeting right after your competitor's presentation has taken place. Having a valid purchasing reason to talk to prospects is essential.

Always have a valid purchasing reason to talk about

It is vital that you keep a dialogue open all the time and have a valid purchasing reason to discuss with your prospect. You can't expect someone to want to talk to you if you are calling them up to have a chat about the weather. The reason why I call this a valid purchasing reason, and not a valid sales reason, is to make you think about why you are calling - from the prospect's point of view.

Creating valid purchasing reasons to engage

Make sure some information that your prospect needs can't be too easily accessed without your help.

You might, for example, have a number of case studies for your prospect that were discussed during a demo which they would be interested in, or there could be an article in a magazine that they want to read. Purposely forget to give them this information in the demo (and make sure it's not on your website) and email it to them in a couple of days, or send it in the post.

Now you have a great excuse to call them up (and you will know by the way they talk to you, and the time they give you, if you are still in pole position). If you pick up bad vibes from the call, or sense that something is wrong, then you need to call your coach and find out what is happening.

If your coach is not forthcoming - you are in trouble with this account. You might find they have just seen your competition, so they were the last one talking to them. Try and get another meeting and reinforce your message.

> It's really important that when you arrange another meeting that there is a good *purchasing reason* for it. If you don't have a valid reason, then don't have the meeting.

If you can't think of a valid purchasing reason then utilize the Multi-Level Selling technique of hole 8. See if your presales person has a good reason to visit the prospect, for example to gather information for a more detailed presentation or to clarify a particular point. This is yet another example why you just can't run on too many deals. Think about it, if you are running on too many accounts you can't possibly give the prospect the appropriate amount of time. Now imagine that your competition only has this one account to sell to, who is going to cover the account better?

Spending time with lead sources is just as important as prospects

Last one through the door is just as important when it comes to lead generation. One of the best marketing companies around in the AS/400 days generated more business for themselves not because they had the best product but because they had many people talking to the main lead source.

On the tee

Back in the early days of JD Edwards, IBM was the key to success as the hardware was selected first and then the software. One of our main competitors recognized this and would have a sales rep working out of IBM's offices in all the major branches. As an IBM software supplier you were also expected to help sell and promote IBM's hardware and this competitor certainly led the way there.

We were starting to see more and more accounts with this competitor's name on the shortlist which was not surprising as the IBM sales reps were well aware of the company as they shared the same office and therefore would always recommend them.

We had to react and I employed an IBM person just to sell hardware and visit all the IBM branches. Initially it cost us money but it opened up a number of key contacts at IBM where (eventually) we were looked upon as good guys, and it was not long before leads flowed our way.

Another tactic this competitor used (when they got down to a shortlist of two) was for their CEO to request a meeting with the key technical and economic buyers the day before they were scheduled to meet with us.

At this meeting he would sit down and just cut a deal there and then. He would get them to make a commitment on the understanding that they would be the preferred suppliers and in return they would discount their software by 50%.

The next day we would get a message that the prospect had made a decision for the rival vendor and they were cancelling our meeting. The last one through the door had won!

Losing a deal in this manner only happened once to us as the competitor had a far weaker product and they knew that price was the only card that they could play. So when we bid against them from then on we would explain very early on in the sales cycle what they would do, and qualify the prospect if they were buying a solution that was good for the company or just a cheap deal.

The next time our competitor tried to pull this off, the prospect was ready for this close, and we never lost again to this tactic.

Will they go down the pub?

The best time you can spend with any prospect is in the pub. Let me explain.

The Chequers Inn at Woburn Common helped to close a great deal of business for us at JD Edwards, as did Renso's in Kingsway, London when at Insight Database Systems. When working on a 6 month plus sales cycle you will definitely build up friendships along the way. Some will actually survive long after both parties have left the jobs that brought them together.

These friendships will start with a drink after a demonstration and will lead to a round of golf or a ticket to see England play rugby at Twickenham. Having a great office with a good pub or restaurant nearby will differentiate you from the competition.

On the tee

We were selling to an up-market retail store with offices in Hong Kong, New York and London. It was a big deal for us as it was a really prestigious name and there were a number of sites that were going to take our software.

The main decision maker, James, was based in Hong Kong and I had met him there a number of months previously. They used our software in Hong Kong but now wanted to buy in the UK. James had moved back to the UK.

He walked into the demo room. It was a competitive bid against all the usual suspects but when he entered the room he gave me a handshake and a pat on the back like a long lost friend. "How are you doing Nick? It's great to see you again."

Why we had to go through the sales cycle I just don't know as this deal was already done, but I suppose it was for the benefit of the people who had not seen our software in the UK.

Anyway, one day after one of the demonstrations, we finished around 5.00pm and James suggested that we should go for a swift half before we went home. So my sales guy, James and I crossed over Kingsway to Renso's (a nice little wine bar). We had a great evening and talked about sport in general, the state of the economy and how Hong Kong was changing. Not a word was discussed about work. We left at 9.00pm and agreed that we would meet up again the following week to go through Accounts Receivable with the team back at the office.

After this Accounts Receivable meeting, the same thing happened (a trip to Renso's) but this time it was 10.00pm when we left the wine bar, and so it went on.

About three weeks through the sales cycle we found ourselves in the wine bar again, but this time my sales guy was looking the worse for wear. "Nick we are going to have to close this deal soon because my liver can't take much more of this and I am going to die of alcohol poisoning," he pleaded with me.

That night James was in trouble and had far too much to drink. One of the presales guys was going home the same way, so we said our goodbyes and off they went to the tube station.

What happened next? James decided to throw up on the tube. He then collapsed and our presales guy carried him home, cleaned him up, and put him to bed.

James did not come into the office the next day, but a signed copy of the contract arrived on the fax.

Now this is an extreme case and I am not saying that you need to get your prospect into a pub, get them drunk and then embarrass them into signing a contract. My point here is that socializing, when it is appropriate, is a necessary step in the sales cycle.

> If you can get your prospect to socialize with you, the chance of a close is far greater.

Don't push too hard

Now you need to be able to gauge whether or not it is appropriate to take someone down the pub, and this comes down to reading the person and determining just how well you are bonding. Something that we learnt at hole 2 "EQ".

There was many a time, after a long day's demo at the JD Edwards' office at Bourne End, when all the staff would say their goodbyes and the prospect's CFO was left just talking to me and the sales guy. It was obvious that he wanted to continue this conversation so it was appropriate to say. "Let's grab a bite to eat and pop up to the Chequers to carry on this conversation. It's one of the nicest pubs in Bucks, you will love it." And up we'd go.

After we had discussed business for a while we then moved on to football and other things, the more personal the stuff we talked about - the stronger the bond we were making.

We had a 100% hit rate when we took key buyers to the Chequers. You have to go there to see just what I mean. If you are based in the middle of an industrial park with high rise offices there is no chance that this part of the sales cycle can be pulled off.

One of the companies I worked at was based in North London, and I moved the sales office to Amersham, partly because I lived just down the road, but also because it's a beautiful town and has a number of very good restaurants and coffee shops where we could take prospects and get them relaxed.

I can remember entertaining an overseas visitor and he said: "Nick, this is a great place. Do you have many theme parks like this in the UK!!!?"

So what happens if you can't utilize this strategy as your office is based bang in the middle of a trading estate with only the canteen to go to? Well there are hundreds of temporary offices around the country where you can hire a boardroom for the morning at a good rate. Why not try this next time when you have a meeting? Find a great location with a good pub or restaurant and suggest to your prospect that you meet there, and then go on for lunch? It will bring a totally different dimension to the deal and you just might find out something that you would not have if you went down to the canteen for lunch.

Some of the no bid tactics that we will use on the 10th hole end up in the pub because this is where you can really have heart-to-heart conversations rather than some brightly lit office that does not lend itself to an informal conversation.

Great EQ

You need really high EQ to pull off going down to the pub because the concept here is to move away from business onto other things and you need to let go of business issues once you've got them out of the way.

I can just imagine how a hard-nosed sales guy with low EQ would bore the buyer to death if all they talked about was how things were going in the sale, what their chances were, and when the deal will close. All this will come out from the prospect without the need for you to prompt matters, provided you develop rapport with them.

> You never need to ask how things are going. You should just know. But so much information will be volunteered if you can get them into neutral territories such as restaurants, coffee shops and pubs.

Not appropriate for all accounts?

Going down to the pub might not be appropriate for some customers. For example selling to local government is hard, as all the buyers are told not to socialize, go on jollies, or play golf with any of the vendors. So don't try to play this shot every time. If you can make it happen, the sales cycle moves smoothly but it does depend on the seniority of the person that you have. You don't want to spend too much time in the pub with "The Weakest Link", for example.

Also watch out for who is paying the bill; if the prospect offers to pay then this could be a red flag. Why? Well they obviously like you but know that the decision might go the other way so they are being nice and want to buy lunch as they feel obliged to do so. If, however, your lunch guest is about to make a decision in favour of your company and is going to spend many millions of dollars on your solution, not only will he want to negotiate the price down but he or she will be happy for you to pay for lunch as well!

Lasting relationships

I still keep in contact with a number of CFOs and CIOs who became good friends, and I have managed to sell to one multinational company whilst working at 4 different vendors over a period of 20 years because of my relationship in that account with past and current CIOs.

Calling on your customers

As your company grows, it becomes very easy to lose contact with your customers and I always tried to put time away for a lunch or dinner with our largest customers. I see it as simple as this - if you don't call on them, your competition will, and if you have built up this great relationship during the sales cycle you can't just drop the relationship once you get the order.

On the tee

One of my best customers (who I kept in regular contact with) rang me up one day. "Nick, we have a competitor of yours seeing our CFO. I need to discuss this with you and we need to make a plan on how to keep them out."

This was a really interesting sales cycle because we were not selling anything, but the end users of our software were not using our software very well, and they were now starting to look at a competitive product.

The CIO recognized that this was an educational issue. He hired a dedicated person to work on our software whose job was to teach all the European divisions how to better use it. It worked a treat and the competition spent 6 months building modifications to their software - trying to break into my account! They failed and if they had a good sales process they should not have even tried. But if I had not nurtured our relationship and simply run away after we had closed the deal, then they might have just cracked this deal.

By the way this is a great example of a defensive strategy that we cover on the next hole.

Sometimes, too much information is a bad thing

There are many times when you could give out too much information, at a meeting or through another means, which could lead to a loss of contact with the prospect. Websites are typical of this, especially if you are embarking on Sales 2.0.

I can remember a time when we were trying to sell to a prospect only for them to say that they "had seen our software and know all about it". They then decided to rule us out of the evaluation.

No one could remember ever showing them our solution but what had happened was the prospect had come to our website and made up their minds that our solution was not for them. Too much information on your website without capturing email details or having software that can monitor who is online is very dangerous. Here is my take on Sales 2.0.

Sales 2.0

Sales 2.0 will help you sell more in a B2C (Business to Consumer) market when you have a commodity to sell. A well designed website with as much information as possible is what you want as - with this type of sale - you will never meet the prospect.

Google rankings, AdWords, videos on YouTube and taking advantage of social media websites are essential to success. However it works differently if you are dealing with Business to Business which is the target market this book is aimed at.

If you are not selling a commodity then Sales 2.0 in a Business to Business (B2B) environment should really be renamed: Lead Generation 2.0, as it has little to do with the sales process but more to do with engaging a prospect to get onto a short list.

Sales 2.0 won't win you business on its own in B2B. What Sales 2.0 will do is bring in more opportunities. Without a good sales process, Sales 2.0 could just mean hiring more people to generate more leads that won't get closed, in effect generating too many rabbits with not enough sales reps to chase them.

Some Sales 2.0 concepts

Ace the Sale is about a process of managing a sale so I am not going into too much detail on Sales 2.0 as there are numerous books and web sites where you can find out more. But here are just a few pointers for you.

- Sales 2.0 *encourages* the building of web sites that have everything you can possibly put onto the web, so the customer can make a decision from browsing the site. This works with Business to Consumer when you are selling a commodity but is very dangerous in a Business to Business environment as you lose an opportunity to *talk* to your prospects.
- Sales 2.0 will ensure that your web site has Search Engine Optimization and Google AdWords so that you can be found. Important for both B2B and B2C.
- Sales 2.0 helps with getting a target list of prospects together by using standard and social media sites like Hoovers, Jigsaw, Spoke, LinkedIn, WeCanDoBiz, Twitter and Facebook. Very important with B2B and B2C.
- Sales 2.0 is useful for monitoring trigger events like new management changes, acquisitions or the raising of venture capital through sites like Google News, Inside News and Venture deal. Then, LinkedIn and Facebook can be used to help find contacts who could possibly help you.

More websites are added regularly to help you with the above so you need to keep an eye open for the best ones.

Sales 2.0 in B2B should be the domain of the marketing department but all good sales reps should have a working knowledge of the major networking web sites. If I was employing a sales rep today, one of the things I would want to see is the number of contacts they have on LinkedIn. Sales reps with very few have not moved with the times, conversely sales reps with too many of the wrong type of contacts – old mates, head-hunters etc….can also be a red flag.

> Sales 2.0 is, in my view, about making sure that sales reps are using the most up-to-date technology on the market today to help find, and then engage with, business opportunities. It won't turn you into a person with high "EQ" though, which is the number one ingredient to becoming a great sales rep.

Summary

Last one through the door wins and if you are not talking to your customers and prospects then you can bet that your competition is.

Having a good purchasing reason to talk to your prospects on a regular basis is essential and if they go down the pub with you, not only are you winning the emotional battle, but these people can end up buying off you time and time again.

Now we are getting closer to 'the decision', you need to make a call on whether you can go on the front foot, defend what you have, get 'part' of the business, or walk away. On hole 10 we will see if we need birdies or pars to win the deal.

The **10**th hole

Do you need Birdies or Pars?

In tournament golf the game doesn't really start until the back nine on the last day. In the sales cycle, by the 10th hole you will really know *how you are doing*. Can you win or are you too far back in the field to make a charge? Do you have the better product? Are the strengths of your company lining up with what the prospect really wants?

On this hole we will lay down the strategy for the back nine and ensure that you get something out of this sale.

On this hole we will cover 6 strategies

- Attack.
- Regroup.
- Fragment.
- Delay.
- Defend.
- No Bid.

What is your strategy?

On hole 7 we covered 'how to review an account' - which is something that needs to be continually done. You have met all the players, had a number of presentations, developed a coach and maybe even socialized down at the 19th with a few of the buyers. You have a sales plan and many actions to follow up on with all the buyers. So realistically you should have a good idea on just how well you are doing. I've said it a few times - if you don't know you are winning then you are losing, and there are only really 6 things that you can do now.

Attack: full on assault

If you firmly believe that you have the best product, great relationships with key people, access to the economic buyer, a compelling event and a coach who is highly regarded by their peers, then you need to drive forward with more presentations, meetings and agree a close process with your coach.

You will now need to submit a detailed pricing proposal plus a commitment to look at a draft contract just to ensure that there are no show stoppers down the road with either. You can establish the timescale to close. The procedures to get the contract signed should be discussed.

> In no way let on to the prospect that you know you are in a dominant position.

Ask your questions with hedged phrasing, such as:

- "If we were fortunate enough to win, what would be the steps that you guys need to do to get this deal closed?"
- "Can I also send you a copy of the draft contract as we don't want any show stoppers to crop up right at the end of the evaluation?"

When you are in attack mode you have to assume that your competition knows they are in trouble - so they will be devising a plan to counteract your perceived dominance. Getting to a close as soon as you can is your objective. If you are winning the account and time drags on, all you can now do is lose the deal.

> Never drag your feet when you are in attack mode. When you are winning you need to push for the close as soon as possible.

Regroup: change the rules

If you feel that you are struggling in the account and the competition has an edge in a product area, you are not getting enough meetings, or you just don't have a great coach - then you need to regroup and come up with a brand new strategy.

We were in this position in the early days of selling OneWorld (now E1) at JD Edwards. We were in trouble as we were selling a brand new product on a platform we had no experience with. So we had to come up with a totally different reason for prospects to buy our software.

On the tee

I can remember closing a very big council deal. We were down to the last two vendors and going through reference visits. We had a handful of reference sites or more accurately "installations" as you could not call them reference sites by any stretch of the imagination.

In the sales processes we had to radically change selling from our strength with the AS/400 product (attack mode), to selling our weaknesses as a positive - an opportunity to buy software that would enable the prospect to leapfrog their competition by installing new and flexible business processes.

I devised a whole strategy around buying software that had issues at the time but which, in a year's time, would become a leading edge product that would give the prospect a clear business advantage. The product would put them way ahead of where they could possibly get to through buying an old fashioned solution. Not to mention the value to them personally by having new and exciting client server experiences that Gartner was pushing at the time. It just might make that CV look good.

This strategy actually worked a treat and you would be amazed how much software we sold. It was however a period of time that my team and I were not proud of as the software did have issues. It was something that we had to do to get JD Edwards from an IBM software house to platform independence and truly open systems.

It is an unfortunate fact of life that, at times, the sales team has to almost act as part of R&D. If you have to wait until the product is bulletproof before you sell it you will probably be dead in the water. The sales team at times has to be challenged with selling leading/bleeding edge technologies which will cause some clients issues. The key is to ensure that R&D responds to them and fixes any problems. World class companies such as IBM, SAP and Oracle have all been in this boat.

Selling your weaknesses as a strength

So, here is our competition coming to the 10th with proven software, loads of reference sites and a track record on open systems but they were still losing to us - the new kids on the block.

Time and again we went through all our weaknesses with the prospect and I can remember putting up a PowerPoint slide with these pros and cons before we went into any sale or reference visit.

Cons	Pros
Very few references	Our software is leading edge and uses client server technology. So today few companies have installed it. But it will give you a competitive edge in a year's time.
Issues with the software	You will be put on Gold support and we will be available 24/7. You will be looked after.
Lack of availability of modules	You can fast track the modules you want. Any company signing up with us now will have priority on the development schedule for the modules they need in the future.
Lack of experience with the hardware	We are working closely with the leading consultancy and hardware firms to benchmark our software on the latest technology. We have benchmarking results that you can see.

Selling your weakness upfront (as on hole 5) really did work for us in those early days. The customer was hearing all the problems directly from us. We knew that our competition was going to flag this up anyway, so our view was "let's get in first".

What we were selling was not software but comfort and vision. Comfort that clients will be looked after, and that clients were special. Comfort that they would be a big fish in a small pond compared to 'just another customer' should they go with competitor A. Vision that the prospect was working with technology that was leading edge and would be great for their CV/résumé, *and good for their company in the long run*.

> Never underestimate the comfort factor. Selling comfort is sometimes more important than the actual product or service that you are selling.

Even bad references were good

We came out of reference visits that were so bad it was embarrassing, only for the prospect to say "Nick, that was not too bad. We can see that the software is getting there."

Unbelievable I thought, these people have so bought into the alternative message that they have already made their minds up to buy even before the reference visit, regardless of how good or bad the software might be.

Incidentally after one visit, which was in Ireland, I went and played golf at Druids Glen with the project leader. This was before they had made their final decision so I was pretty confident that we were going to win this deal.

Changing the rules requires sales reps with high Empathy Selling "Hustler / Artist" components (as discussed on hole 2). Turning your weaknesses into strengths can be done but you need creative people in your team to come up with alternative strategies to change the rules of the game. Prospects who are more likely to 'buy into' rule changes will typically be dynamic and have young management.

On the tee

I was playing golf in our winter league and as I stood on the 1st tee I thought that I recognised one of the players in my group. Anyway we played the first and as we went to the green on the second I said: "John, do I know you? You look familiar."

"You bloody well should," he replied. "You were the guy that sold me that load of rubbish OneWorld," he answered.

"Oh yes." Now I remembered. It was in the very early days when we were having issues. "How did it work out?" I said innocently.

"Well I lost my job over it and six months later I got divorced and my life went downhill from there on."

"Oh I am sorry to hear that John. By the way you can have that putt."

You will be pleased to know that we had a laugh about it all back at the 19th. John is now retired and things panned out well for him as he managed to get another job on the back of his experience of installing OneWorld. All was forgiven… even though John and his partner lost the game!

Fragment: can you get part of the deal

If you feel that your position is not strong on the main offering, is there any way that you could go for part of the deal - to keep you in the game?

On the tee

I am going to give you an example from my own business: RacingWebs.com. I love horse racing and have owned a number of horses over the years. All of them, unfortunately, would struggle to win a donkey derby.

I started a hobby business back in 1999 building web sites for racehorse trainers so that I could get closer to racing. I got some really good accounts like Henry Cecil, Martin Pipe (at the time he was champion trainer), Ferdy Murphy, Willie Carson, Gordon Elliott who won the Grand National and a host of other trainers.

There were not many people developing web sites for racehorse trainers back then but now with all these open source products like WordPress, Drupal and Joomla! - building web sites has become a commodity service. VisAds.com is my main business which is all about video marketing and I now don't compete on web development. I switched to building short videos for racehorse trainers to 'coexist' with the web builders of today.

This is an example of how you can get part of the business. In turn, it gives you an opportunity to up sell later if anything goes wrong with your client's relationship with their web master.

We also managed to do this successfully at JD Edwards when in the early days we did not have manufacturing software. So we teamed up with a company called Marcam in the UK, as they were a supplier of process manufacturing software which we did not have.

Conversely Marcam did not have financial software which we did. So between us we had a complete solution from manufacturing, distribution and financials and we could then bid jointly on accounts, accounts that on our own we would have had to no bid on. We both got part of the deal rather than nothing.

We worked together well for a number of years even having joint sales meetings in each other's offices. When JD Edwards eventually produced their own manufacturing software the relationship ended but we had got into accounts which we would never have had any hope of getting into. Later we even managed to move these accounts totally over to JD Edwards.

> Fragment strategies aim to see how you can get part of the business now, rather than the whole, and keep you in the game rather than lose the opportunity outright.

Delay

This will be the strategy that you need to adopt when your competition is in full attack mode and is winning. They will be trying to close the deal as soon as possible so you need to extend the sales cycle in the hope that something will be discovered further down the road that will put you in a better position.

Agree to some further bench testing of your solution, or if you have a new product that is coming around the corner, now is the time to play that card. Present 'what the future holds' if the prospect waited rather than rushing in to buy now. Even if your competitor has a new release they will be reluctant to show it as this would delay the deal.

Create plenty of Fear, Uncertainly, and Doubt (FUD). Are they really sure that it's a good time to buy with the economic climate as it is? Why not go with a small pilot site first before committing, just in case the solution does not match the problem? Tell them: "We would be happy to do this free of charge just so that you can see the software working before you buy." This strategy will hopefully extend the sales cycle and the competitor is likely to prove reluctant to match this offer which might harm their relationship with the prospect.

Defend what you have

Here you are already the incumbent supplier but you have a totally new product that you are trying to up sell to your customer, but it is a competitive situation as another vendor has a similar solution. If you are losing this new piece of business you need to keep what you have as the new vendor will try to sell as much of their product as they can to them. One of their solutions could be a replacement of your existing product!

More attention needs to be given by your support department to this account plus you need to spend more time with the people that like your product. If you lose the new deal - keeping close to the account will enable you to find out how the new vendor is doing. You will come to realise whether there is an opportunity to revisit this bid in the future when your product offering improves.

If the new vendor is doing well you might want to strike up a relationship with them like we did with Marcam so that you can keep them close to you, as per hole 3 "Know your competition".

The Defend strategy is what can happen if you don't spend time with your customers. You can always be sure that your competition is calling on your customer base all the time. Having a good installed accounts team that looks after your customer base is very important in order to hang on to what you have. More on this on hole 13 "The user reference".

The no bid

Walking away from a deal before you have been told you have lost is a very powerful strategy for two good reasons.

1. It leaves the remaining competition in a position of power over the prospect with nowhere for the prospect to go from a negotiating perspective. They won't like this and will want to keep you in the game for as long as possible.
2. All of a sudden it changes the rules - going from a position of possible mistrust on what *you have been saying in the sales campaign*, to one of total trust. Think about it from the prospect's point of view. If these people are willing to walk away from the deal because they are not sure there is a good fit then what they have been telling us over the sales cycle must be true. Unlike the competition, who has said yes to everything we have asked them, so far.

This is a strategy that needs strong resolve and when I suggest this for an account, a sales rep will often think I have gone mad. The sales guy reckons he is waving his commission cheque goodbye for sure, rather than hanging on to the slim hope that things will pick up if we carry on.

When playing golf as a teenager I would frequently go up to the club and have a bet on a game without having the stake to cover it. Luckily for me I was playing against guys that had more money than golfing skills and subsequently I did not need a part time job when I was studying accountancy at University. We would also have a game of cards, at the end of the round, with the losers trying to win back their money. So I was used to taking chances and bluffing my way to a winning hand.

Gambling taught me something though. Knowing how to bluff and when to walk away. I find it interesting when I look at a number of business people I know who say they 'never gamble'. Yet they have just mortgaged their house, taken out more loans and personal guarantees to keep a business with no hope going. When things go belly up, they lose everything. So you don't gamble then!?!

I am happy with the no bid (when appropriate) and we played this strategy out a number of times at JD Edwards. We won them all.

On the tee

We were bidding for a big drinks distributor against a so called specialist supplier but when we got to the 10th we were in big trouble. No one was really helping us and we were not getting feedback from our coach.

I reviewed the account with the sales rep and the lead presales guy, and we all agreed that we had no clue how we were doing… so we must have been losing.

We also had product issues as we had not got the functionality of our competitor in our distribution software to handle the retail part. None of the other strategies above could be played so I suggested the no bid. This would flush them out and if the call I was going to have with our coach was less than three minutes long, then we would know we had lost and we could try some spoiling tactics.

I made the call, our coach was horrified and he demanded a meeting with us. He came down to Bourne End the next day. He completely levelled with us. “Yes your competition is ahead on product but we are really uneasy about them. We like you guys much better but we have some issues with the software.”

Our lead presales guy took down all the issues and came up with a number of workarounds and a modification that we needed to do for them to get to the same level of functionality. After the meeting we went up to the Chequers Inn where we spent a further hour with our coach.

The next day we had access to the economic buyer and anyone else we wanted to meet, and we won the deal. We had won this as we had better people, and because the prospect had issues with the competition’s sales rep and company. As soon as we were prepared to walk from the deal they realised that they could totally trust us as this demonstrated that we were not out to get the deal at any cost. They bought ‘us’ not the product.

The experience of playing golf and cards certainly came in useful later in life!

Summary

Now you have a strategy, you need to implement it. If you are winning, it is very important to get pricing and terms and conditions to the prospect early on. If you are losing, see if you can change the rules, slow the deal down, or just try to get part of the deal.

So let’s assume that we are in attack mode and on the 11th hole we will find out why complex pricing and strange clauses in the contract can be useful. On this hole we won’t be using the sales concept KISS “Keep It Simple Stupid”, but KICH “Keep It Complex Hard”.

The **11** th hole

Complex Pricing and Clauses you don't need

As we come to the 11th we really need to get the ball rolling on pricing and the T&Cs of the contract. You need to know what you are playing for as it will give you the adrenalin rush you need to hole the short putts.

On this hole we will cover

- Getting your pricing and contract in early will speed up the close.
- Complex pricing helps you to get a higher price.
- Having clauses in the contract that you don't need will help during the negotiating phase of the deal.

Get your pricing and contract in early

Getting your pricing and contract in early will help qualify the deal. If, for example, the prospect doesn't want a copy of the contract or a pricing proposal in too soon, then you have a problem on your hands. Whereas if they say "Yes, no problem Nick, send it in" - the signals are altogether better.

You need to make sure that the contract is being seen by the economic buyer or the legal team if this job has been delegated. If the pricing and contract is just 'lying around', that's a red flag. Maybe the project just does not have the momentum that you thought it had? Getting these documents into the hands of the right people will also speed up the close if you can get the process up and running early.

Complex pricing

At JD Edwards we had a really complex price list which some of the sales guys were not fans of. We had modules, module bundles, casual users, report users, power users, enquiry only users, and then we had packs of users that we could bundle in a number of ways.

"Why can't we just have one price for the software?" was the cry from the sales team. Well, I could see a very good reason.

On the tee

We were selling to a large Scandinavian insurance company and we had won the business but had to go to Berlin to negotiate the deal. It was for 100 users of GL (General Ledger).

We travelled to Berlin the day before the negotiation, so that we would be fresh for the meeting, and arrived early at the company's office. When we entered the boardroom we all shook hands, and took our places opposite one another. One of the prospect's team members had been our coach throughout the sale so it was a very relaxed atmosphere. After the pleasantries Don (the sales rep) got down to business.

He stood up and went across to a white board.

"So you will need the financial modules," he began, "but you will also need fixed assets which means that you can take this as a bundle, which is slightly more than the financial module on its own but cheaper if you were to add fixed assets as well. You will also need some casual users and, oh by the way, how many power users do you want?"

I looked at the two guys opposite me, and even on a low EQ day, it was quite clear to me that they had no idea what my colleague was saying. Come to that I was struggling as well.

"Hold on, hold on," I cried. "Can I just take a time out here? Do you guys understand what is going on up there?"

"Not a clue," was the reply.

I turned to my colleague. "Look, I am confused Don. So I am going to pretend that I am on the side of these guys."

I moved my chair around the table to join the other two.

This was a very important move as it symbolized that I was now on their side. There were now the two buyers and me against Don. "Why don't you try again?" I suggested. So off Don went and tried to explain our pricing for the second time.

.

After a few minutes, I piped up again. "Okay, this in not working," I said. I think the prospects were pleased that they had another member of the negotiating team on their side.

I took the lead. "Can I ask you guys how many users are you looking for?" I said.

"100," was the reply.

"Okay, what sort of budget have you got for this purchase?"

"Oh around $1m."

"Right wipe all of that off the board Don, and put up two numbers. 100 and $1m."

I turned in my seat and faced my new colleagues. "Is this okay with you guys?" I asked.

"Yes, thank you Nick."

And that was that. We got the contract signed, with about $300k more than we thought we were going to get and Don and I spent the afternoon at the Checkpoint Charlie museum before flying home. I love Scandinavians; it's the only deal I negotiated from both sides!

Complex pricing is good for negotiating

The trip to Berlin taught me a very important lesson; complex pricing is good for negotiating. Complex pricing is fantastic for getting a higher price. If we had started off saying that 100 users would cost $1m - where do you think we would have ended up? At the $700k mark. We would then have had to find another deal to make our numbers.

Back at The GL Company I purposely built a pricing structure similar to the one at JD Edwards. Once again the sales force was upset that we did not have something simple in place. This price list ensured that we became a really profitable business as we got very high prices but more importantly we always based our maintenance on the list prices and rarely discounted that. Maintenance is the crown jewel of a software deal as it goes relatively unnoticed from year-to-year once you have signed up the client, with the added benefit of no more selling and approvals to go through.

Customers will always want a discount on whatever price you start off with. Aim high and you will get a good price. Drop the price list, and you will still end up having to discount. Then you will need to find more business to make your numbers. It's an obvious thing to say but if you can reduce the amount of discount you give, the less you will have to sell. But how many times do we really achieve this? Think about it - if we only got $700k for our deal in Berlin we would have needed to find an extra $300k from another account. This would mean another sales cycle, more time taken up, more expense for the company, and we would never have seen Checkpoint Charlie!

Multinational user price

If you are dealing with a multinational account then prices for your products or services could vary from country to country. At JD Edwards we based our prices in local countries on the Big Mac index.

1. Firstly work out the price in US dollars. Now reference the cost of a Big Mac at McDonald's in the US as the base price.
2. Then work out how much a Big Mac would cost in US dollars in each country you sell in.
3. Divide this cost by the US cost and use this number as the Big Mac factor to work out your local price.

This new price list can only be used if the prospect is a local company buying only in the target country. However what happens if a multinational company based in one of these territories wants to purchase outside of their country, or better still outside the continent? The best way around this is to have a multinational price list which is 20% higher than the US dollar price list.

You can justify the reason for this higher price through an explanation that the cost of doing business in multiple locations is higher as there is a need to demonstrate products or services in multiple locations and a requirement for foreign language support. This is a good negotiation chip (a negotiation chip is an instrument that we will be discussing in detail on hole 17 "Negotiation").

What might happen is that you end up having to negotiate off the local price list of the country that the contract will be signed in (if a prospect asks you about local pricing – there is no point denying the existence of such a price list if it exists). But if you had started off from this price list first you would have had to discount even more, so this is another great tip to maintain a higher price.

Small company pricing

Down at the other end you need to recognize that small companies can become larger ones and you could devise a price list around a few users only, the size of a computer processor, or the turnover of the prospect. This way, as they grow, you can then increase the price which protects your margin.

> Use your imagination to devise a number of price lists. It will help you maximize your revenue and assist with negotiations.

These tips are hard to implement as a sales rep and they need to be discussed at management meetings if they are to be implemented in your company.

Putting in clauses that you don't need

The 17th hole is all about negotiation and it's a fun hole. But you can tee yourself up early for the 17th by putting in clauses that you can live without, or terms too favourable to you, as a negotiating tactic.

When the prospect gets an internal lawyer involved you can add two months to the sales cycle. If they use an outside lawyer then three months plus! Remember "internal politics" impacts upon everything. Lawyers need to be seen to be doing a good job and an outside lawyer is printing their own money if they can come up with issues that drag on. This is why it's so important to get contracts and pricing in early - as they will slow down the close.

Clauses to add in

Here are a number of clauses that you might want to consider utilizing tactically.

Publicity

This is always a great clause that you can make a big deal about. At The GL Company we wrote a whole section on what customers would do once they had signed. A case study, for example, plus they would agree to be referenced on our customer list on our web site.

Every time this came up as an issue we negotiated this away as a concession. Customers want good relationships with their vendors and you will always get reference visits and help without this clause. Make it look like a big concession and you just might save an extra point or two on the discount at the end of the negotiation. It might even distract them from some of the other clauses!

On the tee

We were selling to a large pharmaceutical company that never let any of their suppliers put their name on user lists, or publicly announce that they were a customer of a particular vendor. When they saw the publicity clause in the contract they were so outraged that they just focused in on it. I got a call from the buyer. "Nick we have a really big problem on one of the terms in your contract, we need to see you." Ok I thought, this sounds like a problem.

So off I went with my sales rep to go through the contract. When we arrived and the pleasantries were over we asked what the problem was. We then got a lecture from the buyer about our publicity clause. "Did you know that we never endorse any vendor? We have a major show stopper over this publicity clause of yours. Not even IBM would get this clause through."

Inside I was laughing, *thank God for that*, I thought that there might be a *real* show stopper. Having observed just how wound up the guy was I thought that I would spin things out a bit more. "But it is so important for us to have a company of your reputation and size on our user list. Is there no way we can just have your name on our user list and we can forget about the case study?" I asked.

"No this whole clause is untenable."

I thought for a moment as I did not want to answer too quickly and said: "Okay what about the rest of the contract?"

"We are fine with all the other points," was the reply.

"Okay. Then in return for a signed contract this week we will just delete this whole section for you. I am really sorry to see how upset you are, and can totally understand your position."

We shook hands, left on good terms, and we never even discussed payment terms - which is my next point.

Payment terms

Aggressive payment terms is another clause that you should have. 75% on contract signing and 25% on delivery of the software normally gets some attention at the negotiation stage. Moving on this could help with other issues that you can't move on.

Attending the user group

This is another clause that you could put in and which can be negotiated out. What this clause would do is to stipulate that at least two employees of the company would attend the annual user group.

I am sure that if you look through the contract that you use today you might be able to come up with a few sections that can easily be negotiated away. Well then, make them more prominent!

Why getting in your pricing and contract will speed up the close

Let's return to the broad point about pricing and contracts. Don't miss a chance to get your pricing and contract in early. As I said at the beginning of this hole - it's a great qualifier - but more importantly if you have done this early and things have been reviewed by the right people you can forecast business with greater accuracy.

On the tee

When I took over the sales and marketing at one of the companies I worked at, we had a few deals kicking around courtesy of the existing sales force. The sales cycle was not a long one as we were selling sandwiches (Hole 4) which meant the initial sale could be signed off without board approval. My first forecast meeting was interesting to say the least.

"So what are we going to close this month?" I asked.

"Well I think we will do X," was the reply.

"Okay, let's have a look at the details then."

No contract had been sent out and they had not even put in a formal pricing proposal but it was forecast to close that month. So there was a bit of re-aligning of expectations from both sides and the need for a sales process to be put in place quickly, with some education on why getting the pricing and contract in early was essential.

This is why it is so important to have an appropriate section in your CRM system. You can see that all the basic stuff like pricing and contracts have been sent, discussed, and entered into the system.

Both parties know why they are in dialogue with each other, so don't be afraid to suggest that the contract and pricing is dealt with early in the sales cycle. You just need to phrase it correctly.

"It might be a good idea to run the pricing and contract through your side now, just in case we are fortunate enough to win you business. We don't want a silly clause or a pricing hiccup to cause problems at the end of all this hard work we have done together."

Summary

Having a complex price list enables you to start off at a higher price than if you had a simple one. Don't be frightened of a high price as a high price means *quality*. You will be negotiated down… as we will see on hole 17.

Having clauses in the contract that you don't need enables lawyers to look like they are earning their fee, plus they distract from the real clauses that are non-negotiable.

Getting your pricing and contract in early will help speed up the close and help qualify matters if there really is any urgency to move forward.

We are now ready to head to the 12th were we will talk about a topic that is seldom discussed: "internal selling". When you observe some of the best sales reps in operation they spend as much time selling to their own staff as they do to the prospect. Let's find out why!

The **12** th hole

Internal Selling: why is it so important?

If you don't adhere to the dress code, go off the wrong tee, and don't know golf etiquette then even if you play off scratch, you won't get many games and will not last long at your golf club.

To be a top sales person you need to rely on the resources that your company gives you. If you can't muster the best presales resources, high level management time, technical and admin support to help you, then you will be a loner struggling to hit your numbers.

What we will cover on this hole

- Why to cover internal selling.
- Everyone sells.
- Sincerity is the key.

Why hole 12

You have done everything right so far. You have a great relationship with the prospect, your coach is telling you what is going on, and things are looking good - but when you try to book some technical resources you find it hard to get anyone.

Angrily you storm into your manager's office. "Look I am going to win this deal but I can't get any resources. You'd better get Danny to step up to the mark pretty soon, or I am going to throw my toys around."

Danny does the demo but he is not happy. His body language is negative and he does not seem as enthusiastic about the product as he should. The deal looks to be slipping. It's not your fault though, it's everyone else's. Or is it?

The reason why I am tackling this topic on the 12th is because a sales rep has got everything right so far. The rep understands the sales process, uses the CRM system well, has a plan for all the buyers, and is on an attack strategy. Things are falling down because the rep doesn't realise that selling internally is just as important as external selling.

I have seen a number of talented sales reps come across fantastically well in front of the prospect but very badly in the office where they treat the people they work with as if they are just factors of production that are there to help them make money.

Hole 12 might just make a few people think, and take stock on how to treat people in their own company.

Everyone sells

At JD Edwards the first port of call was our receptionist, "Patty", who was simply the best. She greeted everyone with a smile, got them tea and coffee, and engaged in conversation. By the time the prospect came into the demo room they had already made up their minds that this was a company with which they could do business. Patty had made a sale before they had seen a single screen of our software.

> Prospects will meet many people in your organization. Everyone they come into contact with is 'selling'; everyone they meet needs to be looked after and treated accordingly.

Presales are king

In the ERP market the guys that present the software can make or break a deal, and this was why (at JD Edwards SUMA region) they were the highest paid people in the industry.

Now this was not something that was directed down from the Denver HQ. It was because I was lucky enough to have some of the best sales reps working for me. They all recognised that the presales people needed looking after. My sales team were good at internal sales, they realised that looking after people meant that *they* would be looked after.

Keep people doing what they are good at

How many times do you see someone who is a great product presenter/demonstrator wanting to be a sales rep because they can make more money? A great presales person can service many sales reps but as soon as that person moves into sales you have lost them from the team. I could replace a sales rep relatively easily but a good presales person with many years of experience is almost impossible to replace. So how did we keep them happy?

On the tee

Every year I was allowed to hand out pay rises of a certain percentage across the sales and presales team. I sat down with the sales team and discussed the importance of keeping the presales team where they were, and they all agreed that they would not take any rise in basic salary. The sales team was confident of making this up in spades with commission.

We managed to do this for three years in a row without Denver finding out. What this meant was that our presales team were so well paid that they had no thoughts of going into sales - far from it. They worked all hours under the sun and were grateful to the sales team for this fine gesture which recognised their importance to the team.

We also had a rule that a presales person would never buy a drink if a sales rep was in the bar and any really expensive toys would be parked in another car park. It really is depressing if you are key to a sale and as you walk into the office you pass a row of expensive sports cars. This also sends the wrong message to the Prospect – "what *no discount*, even though the car park is full of Porsches and BMWs"?

Sincerity is the key

"The key to success is sincerity. Once you can fake that, you've got it made."

Joe Franklin the famous New York talk show host claimed that he was the person that coined this phase on the very first "This American Life" but actually this quote was initially coined by Jean Giraudoux who suggested: "The secret of success is sincerity".

Jean was a French novelist, essayist, diplomat and playwright and had this to say about golf. "A golf course is the epitome of all that is purely transitory in the universe; a space not to dwell in, but to get over as quickly as possible."

Well I might just agree with him when I am having one of my bad rounds but I absolutely get the point about sincerity. It would be nice to be genuinely sincere in all your business dealings. But how many times are you sitting in a meeting wanting to throw a cup of coffee all over your boss, or tell a prospect they are talking total crap?

We have all been there and instead of throwing coffee the words that come out are: "Great idea Bill. Totally agree," or "Yes, that's a good point I will make a note of it."

You then throw away the piece of paper when you have left the meeting, and do the total opposite.

I think the best approach is to really appreciate other people's points of view or seek an understanding of how they are behaving. If you have ever studied NLP in any depth one of the presuppositions is that "people are not their behaviours". Accept the person and see if you can change their behaviour. This is what a great sales person is trying to achieve, to get into a rapport with a prospect - a state when they are in agreement with what you are saying.

If you can train your mind to do this and treat everyone with respect and understand that people see things from different perspectives, you will achieve much better relationships which ultimately will lead to sales. Of course, this applies not just to your prospects but to everyone that you interact with.

Help required

As mentioned above, I have seen a number of very good sales people who are great in front of the prospect, and do everything right. But as soon as they leave the meeting they call up someone in the office demanding instant action! Or worse still, having asked for help, they then ask another person for exactly the same thing - after they have put the phone down to the first person.

Certain sales people think they will get the information they need more quickly if they use the shotgun approach. But the people whose help has been called upon are in the same office. They talk to each other and will come to the conclusion that they are 'not to be trusted' to do what the sales guy has just asked them.

Word gets around and the next time someone is asked for assistance, it goes right down to the bottom of their to-do list. Before you know what has happened you have such a low rating internally that you can't get things done. "I can't believe it. Everyone is useless in this company. I have to do everything myself," is the normal response when you can't sell internally. It's always someone else's fault, but never yours.

Think about who is key to your success and make sure that they are being well looked after. If you have no influence on the money they earn you can show them genuine respect by never taking what they do for granted.

The sales rep who has a low internal rating will often have high Empathy Selling Hustler and Politician components which we discussed on hole 2 (EQ). The Hustler component makes the sales person come across as sincere in front of the prospect as he knows he needs the order to get the commission. But when the rep comes back to the office they don't have to act sincerely anymore, so when they need any help to answer an ITT or for someone to do a demonstration - they just *demand* action rather than asking in a respectful way. Well other people are just employees after all (goes the thinking) and should be doing their job anyway. And what might that be? Making our sales rep with the low EQ money.

These types of sales reps are very hard to manage; they constantly bring in their numbers but cause havoc internally. They need to play hole 2 again and again. They need to see that internal selling will bring them more money with less hassle and this will curb their behaviour to some extent. I find it hard to manage people like this, and the only way I can get people to work with them is to tell this little story.

The scorpion and the frog

One day, a scorpion looked around at the mountain where he lived and decided that he wanted a change. So he set out on a journey through the forests and hills. He climbed over rocks and under vines and kept going until he reached a river.

The river was wide and swift, and the scorpion stopped to reconsider the situation. He couldn't see any way across. So he ran upriver and then checked downriver, all the while thinking that he might have to turn back.

Suddenly, he saw a frog sitting in the rushes by the bank of the stream on the other side of the river. He decided to ask the frog for help getting across the stream.

“Hellooo Mr. Frog!” called the scorpion across the water, “Would you be so kind as to give me a ride on your back across the river?”

“Well now, Mr. Scorpion! How do I know that if I try to help you, you won’t try to *kill* me?” asked the frog hesitantly.

“Because,” the scorpion replied, “If I try to kill you, then I would die too, for you see I cannot swim!”

Now this seemed to make sense to the frog. But he asked. “What about when I get close to the bank? You could still try to kill me and get back to the shore!”

“This is true,” agreed the scorpion, “But then I wouldn't be able to get to the other side of the river!”

“Alright then... how do I know you won’t just wait till we get to the other side and THEN kill me?” said the frog.

“Ahh...” crooned the scorpion, “Because you see, once you've taken me to the other side of this river, I will be so grateful for your help, that it would hardly be fair to reward you with death, now would it!?!”

So the frog agreed to take the scorpion across the river. He swam over to the bank and settled himself near the mud to pick up his passenger. The scorpion crawled onto the frog's back, his sharp claws prickling into the frog's soft hide, and the frog slid into the river. The muddy water swirled around them, but the frog stayed near the surface so the scorpion would not drown. He kicked strongly through the first half of the stream, his flippers paddling wildly against the current.

Halfway across the river, the frog suddenly felt a sharp sting in his back and, out of the corner of his eye, saw the scorpion remove his stinger from the frog's back. A deadening numbness began to creep into his limbs.

"You fool!" croaked the frog, "Now we shall both die! Why on earth did you do that?"

The scorpion shrugged, and did a little jig on the drowning frog's back.

"I could not help myself. It is my nature."

Then they both sank into the muddy waters of the swiftly flowing river.

Self destruction - "It's my Nature", said the Scorpion...

* This version of *The Scorpion and the Frog* has been reproduced with permission from http://allaboutfrogs.org/stories/scorpion.html

I once had a sales rep who behaved exactly as outlined above. What I was able to do was neutralise the individual as I got the people who worked in our company to *understand that he was a scorpion and could not help himself.* So I sold around him and he got help not because of his internal sales skills (or lack of them) but because people understood how he was made up and felt sorry for him. After this he was known as the scorpion sales rep.

The red button

Sometimes you need to tell a team member that they are doing something wrong. Criticism is not a great thing to offer as people don't like it. This is how we managed one particular situation.

We were just launching our distribution software at JD Edwards and we had no formal presales person, so we were using this really enthusiastic consultant – Steve – to do the demos.

When we got to the architecture of the software he would always introduce this as the most complex part of our software. "Yes this is really complex," he would say, "and it took me a long time to get to grips with it."

At one demo, the sales rep was fuming, and what was worse - Steve was not looking at him. If he had, Steve might have picked up the body language which would have been self-explanatory enough to indicate that he was making mistakes. He also started to re-explain things after the prospect had got the point 5 minutes earlier which put doubt back in their minds.

So after the demo the sales rep, Lenny, sat him down and explained about the red button. "Steve, you did a great job but you need to look at me because there are times that you need to *move on* in the presentation. Remember we are here to sell, not to install."

Steve started to look a bit depressed. Lenny continued: "Also you need to watch what words you use. For example, complex is one of those words. Moreover, please do not describe our software architecture as the most difficult part of the software to understand; describe it as leading edge and the key features allow you to do X."

"Okay," replied Steve. "But how am I going to remember this? There is so much to learn."

"Steve what you have to imagine is that there are two electrodes attached to you. The wires run under the table and are attached to a big red button which is just in front of me when you do your demonstration. Now this button is linked to 25,000 volts that will be released if I press the big red button."

Steve was looking worried.

Lenny continued. "Now all you have to do is look at me when you are answering a question and next time we talk about architecture words like 'complex' and 'really difficult', well that will make me press the red button."

Steve got the joke. From then on everybody knew about the red button and the next time Steve did a demo I asked Lenny how it went. "Great," he said. "I only had to press the red button once."

How much better is that than giving Steve a roasting over how he did the demo? A roasting would have been demoralizing and probably would have failed to get the point across. Now every time Steve did a demo, we would go in and simply say: "Watch the red button, Steve."

"Okay!" was his reply.

> When giving new employees negative feedback or criticism, it can be demoralizing for the employee. If you can get your point across in an amusing manner it deflects the feeling of failure and can be mentioned without fear of upsetting them in the future.

Answering Invitations To Tenders (ITTs)

I hate doing these, and I am sure that you do as well; answering hundreds of questions does not appeal to most sales people. This is where internal selling really comes in. You need someone else to do them for you especially if you have a low "E" (Engineering component) in your Empathy Selling profile.

People will genuinely want to help you if you can sell to them. If you are good at internal selling you will find that there are many people who are prepared to help you, even within the sales team where there is competition. Get this wrong however and people will go out of their way to put obstacles in your path. If you can get a sales team that pulls together and wants everyone else to succeed this will lead to a great atmosphere in the sales team which will lead to everyone succeeding.

How to get people on your side

- Get them involved. When you have an account review, ask for people's input. The presales person has had more face time with your user buyers and will come up with some good ideas and strategies. Take them on board and be seen to implement them. Asking people for advice is a great way of making them feel important.
- Write a great email and copy their boss in on it. There is nothing better than your boss getting an email from someone singing your praises. "Chloe, I just want to say what a great job Steve did in the latest demo to XYZ Company. Without doubt we are now in pole position thanks to Steve." I bet you Steve now wants to win this deal more than you do.
- If you have a *big win* take out the key people for a good lunch or dinner and show them how much you appreciate their help.

Summary

Being able to sell internally is just as important as selling to the prospect and the really great sales reps do both. If you genuinely respect what other people's roles and responsibilities are, and treat people well, you will find that you will be repaid.

Here are my rules of thumb:

1. Respect your colleagues.
2. Ask for their help.
3. Praise people when they have done well.
4. Use humour when they make mistakes.
5. Be genuine.

Okay, well we are nearly finished with all the presentations and we now can play the 13th which is the final presentation before the prospect makes up their minds.

The **13**th hole

The Final Presentation

The final presentation represents the last chance to see most of the buying team before they make their decision. What do you need to do? What should you say? Do you need birdies and eagles or just a few pars to close this deal?

On this hole

- Tactics when you are winning or losing.
- "It's all about them".
- Leave them with *three reasons*.
- Make sure that you have another meeting.

Are you winning or losing?

I am going to divide this section in two, based on whether you believe you are winning the deal, or losing it.

Think you are winning?

You know that you are winning this deal so you don't need to take out your driver, you just need pars. The final presentation should be an iron off the tee, a second shot onto the green, and two putts.

Be prepared for your competition to have thrown all the muck they can at you as they know that they are losing. But, by selling your weaknesses upfront, you have nothing to fear, do you? Or have you forgotten one or two things that you should have mentioned?

Your coach has briefed you on all the players and what you need to do. You have great relationships with all the buyers. You know all the hot buttons that have made the buyers want your solution so this last presentation should be a breeze. In reality, you only get a handful of deals like this, most of the time you will be going into the last presentation a bit apprehensive (even if you are confident of coming out on top) and so you should.

An overconfident sales rep is a red flag. In my selling career, if everyone tells me that we are winning - I won't believe them until the contract is signed and the money is in. Don't forget that everyone lies to you, you just can't be sure.

England 2018 World Cup bid

There was no better example of people lying to you than the failed bid of England's 2018 World Cup. Towards the end of the sales cycle we had David Beckham, Prince William and David Cameron all trying to secure first round votes, and then gathering support for the second round as no one was expecting a winning majority first time around.

A key strategy on England's bid was to cultivate FIFA's high-ranking Trinidadian executive member Jack Warner who would deliver the all-important three CONCACAF (the Confederation of North, Central American and Caribbean Association Football) votes. Warner ultimately failed to deliver during the secret ballot in Zurich.

It's like getting your CEO, COO and CIO to spend time on an account with the key buyers and getting reassurances that they are going to select your solution to then find it rejected. I don't think the sales rep would have a long term career after that.

What's interesting is that England never had a hope in hell of getting this bid as the FIFA president, Sepp Blatter, had gone on record to say that he wanted to give the World Cup to developing nations. *"It's my philosophy to drive forward the expansion of football. The next regions that we need to conquer would be China and India,"* stated Blatter.

Add to this all the speculation of bribes and corruption, and this deal was never going to be successful from day one.

England's two-year campaign to host the World Cup cost an estimated £15 million. If they had put a sales process in place they might have saved some time, money and the embarrassment of making the future King of England look a bit silly. By no bidding you could have played some great golf courses for £15 million.

If there was a sales process in place you would have asked this question first. "What are the buying criteria?" Answer: to give the World cup to developing nations.

So you are right to be apprehensive - if people will lie to our three famous musketeers then they just might lie to a sales rep. Does your coach really have the clout they say they have? Have you really covered off all the buyers in the deal, and do you really know what's in it for them if they buy your solution? Is there a hidden agenda that you have missed or worse still is someone being bribed?

On the tee

Fortunately for me I have seen very few dishonest deals in my career. Sometimes when a decision is made that goes against all rhyme and reason there might have been some skulduggery at play but the only time I saw it for real was when we were jointly bidding on an account with another supplier. We were at the prospect's office for the final presentation. It was all going really well and it was obvious that we were going to win.

I was in the kitchen making a cup of coffee and the CIO came up to me: "You know Nick, the last time I bought software off XYZ company (who was our competition) I got a nice little car for my wife."

I just did not know what to say, so I simply said "Oh really," and carried on making the coffee. We won the deal without having to be dishonest but I was prepared to lose it rather than playing his game.

A number of years later this competitor company went into receivership and one of the directors got arrested for fraud. Now there is not much you can do about dishonesty in a sales cycle except to recognize that it exists and plan around it. You need to get as many people on your side so that the one dodgy vote can't lose you the deal.

Espionage

Espionage. It has been known to happen. Some companies will bend the rules to breaking point in order to get the jump on others. I'm not saying it is commonplace, but there will be times when things feel out of place, your radar goes up a notch, and you need to take additional precautions.

On the tee

At JD Edwards we were on the bid team of one of the big consultancy firms - bidding for the National Lottery's back office systems. When the team leader came to see us he spent most of his time saying that our office could get bugged and explaining that our phone calls could be monitored. "You need to shred anything to do with this bid as people will be going through your dustbins to find anything connected with it," he stated. It was like something out of a spy film, and he was absolutely serious. Scary Hollywood stuff and I am pleased to say that after a few meetings we decided we did not have a good fit so we withdrew. I might not be alive today if we had carried on!

What's my point here? Well sometimes things might not be as straightforward as you think and if you suspect one of the buying team of not having the company's interests at heart you won't change their minds. Ask them questions that they just have to say 'yes' to in front of their peers and bosses, which confirms a good fit for your solution. It will then be hard for them to sabotage the decision when they are on their own later and making the decision on which solution they will go with. What I found with the guy that wanted a car was that he said very little in the final demo as he did not want to draw too much attention to himself. Make him stand out!

Anyway hopefully you will not encounter these things but don't be naive about them.

Summing up

The last presentation should be you at your very best. It's like *summing up* in court; it's your last opportunity before the jury goes out to consider their verdict.

It's all about them

Throughout the sales cycle you should have been building a case for why the prospect would want to buy your solution. This is not the time to talk about yourself; it's time to relate everything you have learned about them, to represent *their* business case and why *they* are embarking on this project - with one small twist. The twist being your solution.

Here is a pitch that our biggest competitor used to do at the final presentation before we overtook them as the market leader back in the JD Edwards days.

"We are the biggest and the best. We have more customers and turnover than anyone else."

They would put up charts and slides showing their rising turnover and number of customers. In a nutshell they were saying *if you don't buy from us you must be mad.*

Now if this competitor had turned the presentation around and worked out the business benefits to the prospect of taking their solution - I think they might have been a bit more successful and stayed in business a bit longer.

When putting together a final presentation use the "What's the benefit" principle, as this will really help you see things from the prospect's perspective. Here are some examples.

You can take a perceived strength of yours, such as longevity, and work it into something the prospect sees as a benefit to them.

For example:

We have been in business for over 50 years

> What's the benefit?

Well this means that we understand your business issues and have the knowledge and expertise to help you.

> Okay, so what's the benefit!?!

It means that our solution will cover all your business processes and that we have the people who can implement everything for you.

> Okay, so what's the benefit?

This means that you will be able to implement better business processes that will speed up delivery, reduce stock levels, and increase customer satisfaction with minimal disruption to your organization.

> Okay, so what's the benefit?

You will be a more profitable organization with fewer staff and lower overheads which will make you more competitive, will lead to an increase of X% in market share with a solution installed in less than a year. This will give you an ROI of Y% in a 3 year period.

Now at last we have found something that is about the prospect, and the reason(s) why they should buy your solution. Don't you think you should start off the presentation with this paragraph and then show how it will come about? 'What's the benefit' is a great test for your pitch, just look at everyday life.

How about more examples?

You sell reading glasses

> What's the benefit?

So that you can see. So you are selling *vision*, not glasses. Focus on the benefit of being able to see.

You sell a newspaper

> What's the benefit?

By reading the newspaper, you will be better informed and will have gained knowledge. You are selling education and knowledge.

You sell a TV

> What's the benefit?

You can watch films and sport, and be entertained. You're selling entertainment not a TV.

Start off all presentations with the business benefit of what will happen once your prospect has bought your solution and then explain how this will be achieved by buying your solution.

So by using 'What's the benefit' - this is how the software presentation above might now look.

Point 1.

By selecting XYZ Ltd you will become a more profitable organization with fewer staff and lower overheads which will make you more competitive, will lead to an increase of X% in market share with a solution installed in less than a year. Giving you an ROI of Y% in a 3 year period.

Point 2.

By selecting XYZ Ltd you will be able to service your customers better, reduce stock levels and increase customer satisfaction because you will have installed better business processes like:

- Direct ship: This means that you will deliver directly from the manufacturer rather than shipping it to your warehouse. [(Remember to show real software on how this is achieved.]

Point 3.

By Selecting XYZ Ltd you will be able to implement a tax saving of Z%.

- Reduce tax: a single data model across multiple locations will reduce your tax burden as all the sales belong to the lowest tax rate of the sales company. [Show more live examples].

Point 4.

By Selecting XYZ Ltd you will use the Quick Implementation Methodology that ensures that the system is up and running quickly with minimal disruption.

- Go through the phases of the Quick Implementation Methodology and show why your solution will be implemented speedily with minimal disruption.

And so on…

Show all the key business benefits to the prospect when they take your solution.

Specifics

The example above is just a quick run through of how to bring business benefits upfront rather than talking about yourself, and how *you* have grown from a company of X% to Y% over the last 5 years, and now employ over Z number of people.

Here are 4 good rules of thumb:

1. Don't spend any time talking about your company. Focus on the prospect's issues and concerns. Get straight to the issues and how your solution will solve their problems.
2. Avoid selling to your coach. You know you have a 'yes' there so focus on the other players. Concentrate hardest on the ones you are not getting a yes from, or those that you are unsure about. Protect your coach, don't give the game away that you have a special relationship with one of the buyers. At the same time, do not totally ignore them.
3. See if you can get confirmation from the doubters in the audience and remember to call them by their first names. "Zoe, can I confirm that we have covered the returns to stock issue correctly for you? I know this was a concern that you had?" "Pete are you happy with the foreign currency consolidation issues now that we have gone through them on the software?"
4. Give the doubters the requisite amount of time. They are the ones you need to sell to, not the ones that have already decided on your solution. Remember sell to the people that say no!

Think you are losing?

If you don't know you are winning then you are losing. So if you are going into this last meeting without confidence then assume this is going to be the last time you see these guys. So, what to do?

You need to go through the same process as above with a benefits pitch but firstly you need to have a real heart-to-heart with your coach before the final presentation. After all, the chances are slim that you can recover this deal. You are going to need to shoot under par. You have nothing to lose so when you have gone through the demonstration based on the winning assumption (as above) that you need to do something a bit risky.

The following are tactics that you can use. Some will work but most will fail. I would much prefer to be coming from a position of strength. But by going through these points at least it will highlight what might be thrown at you when you are in a winning position.

On the tee

We were selling to a retail company and we were not confident about winning the deal. We had a few coaches but this was a big company and there were 15 people involved in the deal from the prospect's side. We were down to a shortlist of two against one of our toughest favourite competitors. We were not confident so we had a very candid talk with our best coach and this is what we discovered:

- The CFO (Economic buyer) was on the side of our competition; our main coach was not as powerful as the competition's although we had the user buyers on our side.
- The competition had offered a 60% discount to the CFO in return for being the preferred supplier so the cost of our solution was twice as much as the other vendor's.

What we said to our coach was that the competition had lost 19 out of the last 20 competitive deals we had bid against them, and they were desperate to reverse this trend. They were clearly prepared to give the software away.

We had a list of accounts that we had won against this competitor and we wanted to see what the best way to use this information might be. (Normally you would just pass this information over to the coach and that would be that).

After discussing things further, our coach said: "This is great stuff Nick and I want you to use it." He continued: "If I come up with it, it will look like sour grapes because the others know I favour your solution. Also the CFO is my boss and he already favours the competition because of the price difference. But if you guys bring this up in a professional manner, then after the presentation, when we all meet up next week to discuss who we will go with, I can reinforce this point as it has not come from me. The decision that I will try to ensure we make, is that we buy the right solution not the cheapest solution."

We knew this was a risky strategy and I would never advise anyone to rubbish your competition. But always play to your strengths and the evidence was overwhelming. The CFO just might make a bad decision because of price, so what to do?

We decided to go for it. In the final presentation the sales rep did a great job. He was high in EQ and delivered the PowerPoint presentation in an honest and professional way and said that all of these clients would be willing to speak to the prospect about their decision. We succeeded because we did not just 'do down' the opposition. My sales guy simply stated the situation and the facts in a low key clinical manner.

It worked well and our coach was able to ensure that the right decision was made. He saved face with his boss - it was not his agenda that all these customers had chosen our solution. So he acted like a judge to ensure that this point was taken on board.

20 out of 21 and this competitor had now been buried once and for all as they could not even give their software away to beat us. Price, eventually, was not the buying criteria here.

> Be very careful using the tactic detailed above in a public arena. Normally this is what is passed in the brown paper envelope to your coach, but in this case the coach could not be seen to be the supplier of the information. It would be a brave person to have not chosen our solution after this information emerged - which our coach was able to ensure did not happen.

Has your competition misled anyone?

Losing situations often become *negative* ones which is why you don't want to end up in this position at the final presentation. However sometimes your competition might have misled your prospect and this needs to be highlighted in a professional manner.

On the tee

Another deal. As we were coming to the final presentation we discovered that our competition had said that they were able to do something that we were sure they could not. So we decided to make this an agenda topic and to labour this point at the meeting. We went into great detail on this feature and showed real live software and the benefit that they would get from it. "You really need to see this feature working on live software," we said. In fact it was one of the three reasons for buying our software we left them with. We will review this, "The Three Reasons" in more detail, at the end of this hole.

Anyway, back to the story. When the prospect went back to check things out with the competitor, they discovered that they had been misled. It was the end for our competitor because they had lost the trust of the prospect. It was only one thing they got wrong but the prospect was not to know this. *What else is out there which they have not been honest with us?* As far as the prospect was now concerned everything this competitor had said was a lie.

> You only need to discover one thing that your competition has misled your prospect on, and all trust will have gone. Remember hole 3 (the first meeting)? If you don't sell your weaknesses upfront - your competition will. And the end of the sales cycle is the very best time to reveal things. A time when competitors can't recover.

If you can't send them to heaven then send them to hell

Again a negative strategy but one that you need to know about. Here you tell the prospect what will happen if they don't buy your solution. You will need to sit down and list all the problems that will happen if they decide not to go with your solution.

- Have a list of unhappy customers that use your competitor's solution.
- Timescales that were not hit.
- Search Google for information of companies suing XYZ Ltd, or having issues with the company.
- Financial instability if applicable. Will they be out of business in a year's time? Who will support the prospect when they are gone?

This is what we found many of our competitors trying to do to us back in my JD Edwards days. Thankfully we never needed to use this approach ourselves, as we managed to send prospects to heaven most of the time, although we did our best to set the correct level of expectation when they got there!

Buying business

A number of times your only tactic is to lower your price and this is the start of a Dutch auction. Personally I would not bother, I think if you have followed holes 1 to 12 so far you should be in great shape. Dropping your price is something that gets the prospect's attention but normally not for long.

Leave them with three reasons

I have had many a debriefing with clients and it's really interesting when you ask *why did you buy from us?* You expect there to be a string of reasons, but no. You normally learn that just a couple of things stand out. "We felt you were the better company and we could trust you." Or "the design of your software and the flexibility was what won the deal." So, knowing this, what you really need to do is make sure that when they talk about your company they have three reasons to buy your solution firmly in their heads. That's all you need!

Have them covered up on a flip chart and as you wind down the meeting just say: "before you go I would just like to take you through three key reasons why our proposition will be of benefit to you."

On the tee

On one of our deals all three reasons were the same.

1. Flexibility.
2. Flexibility.
3. Flexibility.

This was because we were competing with a vendor that had no flexibility.

Their software required foundations many metres deep. Then you needed to fill them with concrete and to build your ERP solution. If, halfway through the implementation, you needed to change direction - well you needed to knock the whole lot down and redo the foundations. Interestingly this vendor is still doing very well today as one of the largest suppliers of ERP software.

Anyway, we won this deal. The reason? 'Flexibility'.

Making up your own terminology

When at JD Edwards one of the things that we had was a great architecture to our software. Now the IT guys got it but using the word "architecture" will mean different things to different people so the user buyers of the software thought they were buying construction software! I feel like an NLP teacher on this hole but another presupposition of NLP, of which there are 14, is the map is not the territory, which means that one person's understanding of a word can be totally different to another.

So at JD Edwards we decided to create a word called ActivERA, or something like that, and stopped using words like architecture. You can then define this word to mean exactly what you want. So everyone now is on the same page and this would be one of the three reasons to leave them on as you can bet the competition don't have ActivERA.

I did the same when I was running sales and marketing at The GL Company. I made up three words and trademarked each of them. We had an admin module which I renamed **SoxBridge**, which was great for the auditors and people wanting to know who wrote what report and when was it last run. We turned a boring old administration module that no one looked at, to one of the main reasons why someone would buy our software. The second was **RepQuiry** which was a combination of a paper report and a drillable online enquiry, and then there was **Virtual OLAP** which was a real time OLAP cube built on the Fly.

So the three reasons to buy The GL Company are:

1. SoxBridge to manage all your reports.
2. RepQuiry to be able to have paper reporting with drillable online inquiries.
3. Virtual OLAP to build unlimited multidimensional views of your data in real time and in a matter of seconds.

Make sure you have another meeting

As on the 9th hole, it's vital that you keep on communicating with your prospect. After the final meeting it might be a further month or two before the decision is made. Don't forget there are more holes to play and even if you are losing - the prospect will want to keep you in the game so that they have a rod to hit the other supplier with, over price.

If more meetings come - this will strengthen your position. If it's hard to get any more meetings - you are on your way out.

Summary

The final presentation is your last chance to influence all the buyers at one time, Keep it down the middle if you are in a winning position but use your driver if you need birdies or better. Leave them with three reasons why your solution is the best for them and keep the dialog open with as many people as you can.

We are now ready to play hole 14 - the reference visit - which is independent verification of your solution. Or is it?

The 14th hole

The Reference Visit

You are now on the shortlist of two potential suppliers. All the official presentations are over and you are down to the reference visits. This is where spending time with your customers and having a great support team really comes into its own. Nervous? Well if you have looked after your customers, this is just a tap in, if not it's a tricky 10 foot putt.

On this hole

- Why looking after your customers is so important.
- The value of going blind, letting the prospect pick who they want to see on your user list.
- Don't work for a company with poor customer satisfaction.
- The need to arrange another meeting.

Why looking after your customers is so important

Look after your customers! This might seem like an obvious statement, but it is essential. It's important not just in terms of reference visits but even more important in boosting your chances of up selling. So many companies are so busy selling to new customers (especially when they are 'Crossing the Chasm') that they forget to keep close to their customer base.

Your customers are your best sales people, your customers are your best product managers; they give you great ideas for your product and you don't even have to pay them. In turn, your customers are the easiest people to sell to.

On the tee

JD Edwards got taken over by PeopleSoft firstly, and then by Oracle. When I left JD Edwards and joined The GL Company I kept in close contact with the JD Edwards user base because we sold real time inquiry tools over their ERP database. As we sold to more of the user base, one of the comments I kept getting back from the JD Edwards customers was that they 'did not know' who their sales rep was anymore. They never heard from them and if they did it was some complete stranger who just wanted to sell them something. "It's not like the old days," they would tell me.

I attended an Oracle meeting with a number of JD Edwards affiliates, plus the new person in charge of the affiliate program for JD Edwards (from Oracle). The reason for the meeting was that Oracle did not have a good contact list for the JD Edwards customer base. They got us together and asked: "would it be possible for you guys to share your contact lists so that we can try to pull a better list together?" Unbelievable.

Okay, so I have made my point about losing contact with your customers - how is this helping you, the sales rep, to sell more? How will it help you sell if you work for one of those companies that fails to look after its customers, or in some cases doesn't even know who their customers are?

If you want to make a success of working at a company which struggles to look after customers then you may need to address the issue yourself. Remember what I said earlier in the book? I would rather a sales rep spent time on the golf course with a customer than bidding bad business. Well this is what you should be doing when you are not immersed in running a sales campaign. There really is never a good reason why a sales rep needs to be in the office apart from attending the odd sales meeting, doing demonstrations, and carrying out some internal selling. If you have spare time, invest it in going to see your customers. It will pay dividends.

Not only might you uncover a new prospect or maybe get an up sell but you are ensuring that you can call upon this company for a reference visit when you need it. Remember (on hole 5) the value in calling someone up weeks before you need something? People will be far more willing to help you if you have genuinely invested your time in them as opposed to seeing them because you want to sell them something.

Now I might be getting some stick here because what some managers really want from their sales reps is for them always appearing to be doing some selling activity. However, a meeting here and there with no agenda can develop into a new lead or the discovery of a business opportunity. Also I have no wish to turn a sales rep into a customer support person, far from it, or to tread all over an installed sales rep's territory. What you need to do is to ensure that the installed sales rep and support department are informed of your plans. If action needs to be taken (like a support issue) as a result of your meeting - don't take this on yourself. Delegate it back to the person responsible. Don't forget internal politics here.

> If you go into someone else's account - always get permission and don't make the support manager look bad if you have to report bad news back to them.

Let me take a moment to underscore my point of view. What is better, a sales rep working on 12 deals and winning 4 or a sales rep working on 6 deals winning all 6 plus having the time to cultivate his customer base with great references? The next time you need a reference, ask the people you have bothered to spend time with - they will help you out.

On the tee

I was doing some marketing work for a JD Edwards affiliate and I called up a few of my old contacts. Whilst on the phone I discovered an opportunity for my old company. No one had been in touch with one particular customer after I had left so I called a colleague who was still working at my old company and they closed a new piece of business because of my call.

How to find the problem customers, survey them.

A good way of knowing what your customers are thinking is to survey them. Here are some sample questions from a scale of 1 to 10.

Q1 - How satisfied are you with the product(s)?

Q2 - How would you rate customer service?

Q3 - Are we responsive to your enhancement requests?

Q4 - Do you get value for money from your software maintenance?

Q5 - How would you rate any training you have received?

Q6 - If you had to make the decision again, how likely would you be to buy the same solution once more?

Q7 - Would you recommend our company to others?

It's especially worth considering a bonus payment for sales reps should they hit scores of 7 or higher on questions 6 and 7.

Don't forget a happy customer is one who has had their expectations exceeded in the sales cycle. The sales rep can directly influence customer satisfaction by setting the expectation bar as low as possible in order to make the sale.

> From the survey you will quickly see the problem customers and identify the actions that need to be taken.

The second and subsequent sales are the most important

Anyone can get an initial sale by lying, setting expectations too high, or just getting lucky. The most important sale however is the second (and later sales) that you make to this customer as this is the best indicator of how happy they really are.

> If you don't keep close to your customers then your competition will.
> Manager's tip: If your sales reps' expenses are too low every month then they are not spending enough time with the customer base.

Companies treating their customers badly?

Companies go out of their way to get new customers, bending over backwards to accommodate their requests, adding new features to get the sale, and negotiating win–win deals. But why is it that once companies get them as a customer they are treated so badly?

On the tee

At VisAds.com, I was doing some video testimonials for one of my clients who had a product running over one of the leading ERP supplier's database. I went to see the group accountant at the company (let's call them Acme) and after some 15 minutes talking about what we would cover in the video he then went on to talk about how bad his ERP system was, and how they wanted to change it.

There had been a total breakdown in the relationship between Acme and the ERP vendor. However, when the software vendor discovered that the company was talking to their main rival a team was put together to try and upgrade them to the latest release. At the same time, and unbeknownst to the sales team, Acme was being pursued for allegedly unpaid license fees very aggressively by another division of the same company.

The ERP deal was worth many millions of dollars. The rival vendor had a 'can do' attitude whereas the incumbent vendor was just putting hurdles in the way. I felt like trying to get the CEOs of both Acme and the ERP supplier down to the Chequers Inn to sort it all out!

> Treat your customers like new opportunities all the time and remember it's 10 times harder to find a new customer than to keep the ones you have.

When to go blind

To be a successful sales rep you need to make a good decision on what company you are joining. You can have the highest EQ in the world but if you are let down by the company right at the end of the sales cycle with an unhappy customer base then it will be a short career. Basically if you have joined a company that does not look after their customers, a hit and run strategy needs to be employed, coupled with a good relationship with an employment agency.

I have been very fortunate in my career and have only every worked for one company (in the very early days) that let their customers down. I was on the support desk back then and it was more like manning the desk of the Samaritans. There was nothing I could do but listen to the horrendous stories of why the system was not working, or how the customer had not received the software that they bought 6 months ago.

When I asked the CEO of the company about the missing software he told me that it had not been written yet. "Nick, sometimes we say things we can't do," was his advice to me. Obviously he had read "Crossing the Chasm" before it had even been written.

Anyway, on one occasion I had been on the support desk listening to a customer for over an hour. At the end, though, the caller thanked me over and over just because I had listened to him. He said that he felt much better now. All I did was sympathize with him; this seemed to be enough. I never found out what happened to the caller as I never heard from him again. I just hope he did not go off and take an overdose.

When I left this company and joined an IBM software house I was scheduled to attend their user group for the first time and was really worried about it. From previous experience the only advice I got when facing a user group was don't forget to wear your cricket pads and box (protective cup). So I was expecting a bad day.

I could not believe it. It was a great meeting and everyone was so positive, discussing how they used the software and what they would like to see in the new releases. Every client was happy, every client was a reference. We used this in our sales cycles. Rather than giving the prospect a few names to select from, we simply gave them the whole user list and said, "just pick anyone you want".

This strategy also worked very well at JD Edwards as we had the same committed and happy user base (before OneWorld was released I might add) compared to our competition who only had a handful of reference sites. We found out that these few reference sites were being given free maintenance and the CEOs were being carefully wined and dined. We would point this out to our coach of course, and get the prospect to enquire of our rivals whether they could see any other companies who used our competitors' software. We knew the reference companies well by now.

So at JD Edwards we would give the prospect our entire user base to pick from. In turn we added that we had encountered issues with some of our installations previously, but that we wanted the prospect to know about this. We wanted the prospects to ask existing customers how happy they were now because we sorted out all their problems.

> The best reference customers are the ones where you had the biggest problems. Why? Because if you managed to sort out their problems and did not let them down they will sing your praises much more than if everything went smoothly (which incidentally with an ERP installation never happens).

Giving out our user list out was no gamble but another great sales strategy which blew away our competition.

It is worth noting that too good a reference is a negative one as it does not help the prospect make up their mind. There is no advice on what to do if there are problems, who got called, and how quickly they sorted out the problem. Also if it is too good it is not credible, people know that things rarely work out perfectly.

Volunteer not to be at the reference visit

This is another important strategy if you have great reference sites. The prospect will be much more open and relaxed without the sales rep watching every move. It is important, however, that you attend the meeting to introduce everyone and thank people for their time. But after the introductions are made it's time to withdraw.

The worst reference visit is when the sales rep attends, handles all the questions, and does not pass the ball to the customer. Sales reps low in EQ will totally dominate the call to the extent that they take the role of the customer the prospect is visiting.

If you do end up sitting in on the actual visit - just observe. Whatever bad comments there are, resist interrupting and trying to explain things on behalf of your customer unless specifically asked to do so by the prospect.

Reference feedback

Without a doubt reference visit feedback is really your best source of how you are doing. It amazes me that the prospect knows that you talk to this reference and they are your customer, but will often still prove willing to share detailed and confidential information with them. Conversations that go: "We want to go live on their software in 6 months time, so what modules would you say we should install first?" or "Can we keep in contact with you after we have bought the software?" These are good conversations and will be reported back to you faithfully when you ask how the reference went.

Also, by not having the sales rep in the actual reference meeting itself you are more likely to have much more additional information flowing from the prospect on *whose* solution they will be buying.

Don't work for a company with poor customer satisfaction

This book is all about how to be a better sales rep and how to close more business in a B2B market. As I mentioned before, joining a company that has poor customer relations will not be a long term career move no matter how good you are. Unless you are desperate to earn just your base salary don't join a company that does not look after its customers.

Hole 5 was all about meeting the prospect for the first time and how to qualify the deal. You should use this same process to qualify a new employer. There are a number of companies that I would never join. The best companies to work for are the ones you consistently start to lose business to, or companies which have great customers.

Losing consistently to a competitor

When you lose a deal, you can check out the competition first hand. You can go to the prospect who passed you over and learn a great deal from the debriefing. Here they will tell you all the reasons why you lost and what was good about the competitor.

When I was working for Insight Database Systems and Data 3 we started to lose deals to JD Edwards and the feedback was that their software was integrated, modern and flexible. Flexible enough that it could be changed by the end user. When I got a call from a friend who was working at JD Edwards in the US who explained how they were looking for someone to set up the UK office and whether I would be interested, I did not have to think about it for too long.

JD Edwards was the best 10 year investment I ever made, joining when they turned over just $40m dollars worldwide. I was part of the company as they grew at a compound rate of 60% every year, going through a $3bn flotation and hitting a turnover of over $1bn a year. I learnt a lot and worked with some quality people who I keep in contact with today.

Arrange another meeting

I just wanted to remind you of the next step here again. You need to make sure that you have another meeting with the prospect lined up to discuss how the user visit went and whether there were any questions that came out during the visit.

If there is nothing to discuss or they don't want the meeting it's a red flag, but all being well you should be having a further meeting where they have lots of questions. Questions concerning how they will be implementing your solution! Remember you still have time to do something about the sale with help from your customer and prospect's feedback. At this stage things have not yet gone past the 'point of no return' which we will cover on hole 16.

Summary

To be a successful sales rep your chances increase significantly if you work for a company that looks after its customers. Having a great reference base means that you can let your prospect select the customer they want to see rather than trying to palm them off to one or two selected customers.

Attending but not being involved in the reference visit will mean your prospect will open up more to your customer and you won't be tempted to answer the questions on behalf of your customer. Too good a reference is a bad reference.

If this hole is not too much of a problem for you then you are already working for the right company. If you consistently bogey or double bogey this hole it might be time to look for a new company to work for.

We are now ready to play the 15th - the board presentation. Now that you are certain that you are the preferred supplier, all you can do at this meeting is lose if you get things wrong. Let's find out how to play this hole.

The 15th hole

The Board Presentation

You have been selected as the preferred vendor and all you have to do now is give a board presentation to win the deal. But you think of Jean Van de Velde blowing away a three shot lead on the final hole in the 1999 British Open at Carnoustie. What do you need to do to make sure you don't throw your lead away?

On this hole

- What level? The "Right Level".
- Deliver it informally but prepare 100%.
- Setting you up for the 17th… "Negotiation".

What level? The "Right Level"

As you come to this hole you might be thinking "well I don't normally do board presentations". You look back over your last 10 deals and can only remember doing one or two, if that. This is normal as there will be many times in a sale that you won't actually be pitching to the main board so you may need to adapt this hole.

Instead of the board presentation we can rename this hole to the *very last high level* presentation to the most senior people in the organization. The people who can make this deal happen.

If you are selling to Walmart or Shell you are not really going to pitch to the CEO unless what you are selling is of strategic importance to the company. So you need to pitch to the people who are the "Right Level". That is what this hole is all about.

If, for example, you are dealing with a multi-billion dollar US company and selling only into Europe, then the European SVP and VP management would be the right level. They must however have a budget which they can spend on what they want, without approval from the US. Alternatively, if you were selling a worldwide ERP solution or something that was outside of their budget then the right level would be the HQ board in the US.

The smaller the company the more likely that the presentation will be to the "C" level people, the people that are actually on the board. If however you are not presenting to "C"s then you need to make sure that the economic buyer (the person who signs off the deal) is at this presentation.

Who should attend from your side?

Before I answer this question I want to tell a story about a company that hired the best business consultants you could find. They were struggling and their market share was falling, so the company hired these consultants at great expense to find out what their problem was, and to advise them on how to become more profitable. After six months the consultants came in all excited and said: "We know what the problem is". The CEO was delighted. "What's the problem then?" he asked.

"You are not selling enough," was the reply.

"Oh," said the CEO. "What should we do about it?"

"Sell more," was the answer.

Now without sales you have no business, and what amazes me is that if sales are the most important thing - why is it that so many *managers, owners of companies* and *C level people* spend so little time doing it?

So who should attend from your end? The most senior people that you can get (who are appropriate to be at the meeting) is the answer. On hole 8 we discussed Multi-Level Selling and how you need to make sure that each buyer is covered by at least two people. Therefore whoever covers the most senior player from your side should definitely be there. I would recommend a four-person team in a software sale: the sales rep, the SVP of sales, the CEO of your company, and the project manager who is going to be responsible for implementing the system.

Now remember - when you bring someone into a meeting you *need* to use them. But your CEO probably does not have the detailed knowledge to stand up there and pitch so leave it to the sales rep / SVP of sales to front the meeting. The trick to making the presentation work is twofold.

You need to predetermine:

1. What you are going to say.
2. How to get the team into the meeting - as you need to pass the ball to them a number of times.

The board pitch

The board pitch should have all the substance from hole 13 (the final presentation) but this time you need to make sure that you *do not* go into too much detail. The people you will be pitching to (if you have not already met them) will all be big Empathy Selling "P"s or Politicians. They all have egos and want their own way. So you need to get to the point quickly. Don't get into confrontation with any of them.

During the meeting, if you find yourself getting hammered hard by a particular person it is probably because they have an agenda that the rest of the board might not agree with. Don't forget - there will be tremendous internal politics at this level so you need to neutralize this person by saying "that is a really good question and needs more time to explain. Can we come back to this a little later?" You can then take the difficult person to one side and address the issue.

Now with your coach prepping you plus research on LinkedIn, there 'should' be no surprises. Do your homework on these board members - where did they work before, what did they buy then?

This presentation should be a supportive one and not hostile; you would not have made it to this hole if things were not going for you. But if someone on the board is coming after you and you are constantly saying "I will get back to this later," you are going to lose credibility. If this guy is carrying on with his own agenda despite being batted away, then answer - even if it is "No we can't do that." Show little emotion and don't get rattled. A *NO* is not a weakness unless your body language says it is.

> Remember - it's not *what* you say it's *how* you say it.

Let the rest of the board see that the board member is working to his own agenda and see if you can gather support for your point of view from other board members and then let *them* fight it out, as you sit back and watch. There will always be one stronger character making the decisions and provided it's not the guy causing you grief you should be okay.

Structuring the Pitch

The structure of the pitch should be based on "What's the benefit?" and hopefully if there is a business plan for this project you have already got your hands on it a long time ago, and you know the key deliverables that the board is looking for.

So all the things we discussed on hole 13 should be present but without the *detailed* product demonstration. Remember to leave the board with *three reasons* to buy your software at the end. These three reasons will be all that the board members remember your product by. If you can deliver these effectively and your competition does not, a week down the line the Empathy Selling "P's" will think it was their idea.

"Samantha, who do you think we should go with?" asks the CEO.

"Well I think we should go with XYZ because they have that "ActivERA", breadth of product, and great customer support."

"That's right," replies the CEO. "You make some good points Samantha. The other vendor does not have the same appeal."

Who should deliver the presentation?

As mentioned above, the sales rep (or SVP of sales) should front the meeting, but who should deliver the actual presentation? It will vary of course, as to whoever has the highest EQ, but my call would be the SVP of sales. Now the SVP of sales needs to orchestrate the presentation so that his team are all included in the actual pitch.

"Hi, I am Nick Gomersall, SVP of Sales, and I would like to introduce the team today. Some of you have met them already. Present are Pete (CEO), Ann (Sales Rep) and Dave (The project manager). What we want to do is go through the key benefits to your business of selecting our software to run your ERP solution."

And off you go.

When it comes to the implementation section, for example, reference Dave. Let him explain the key steps but ensure he remains seated whilst the SVP of sales drives the PowerPoint screens. In this way it keeps the meeting relaxed and informal and the SVP of sales as the focal point.

When it comes to commitment you can reference Pete your CEO - "…and this is why he is here today". Then let Pete give a small pitch, again from where he is seated, about how he wants to see this as a successful project and how he will be the executive sponsor on this project.

The presenter should reference the sales rep now and again, making sure you pass her the ball. In my experience I have found this relaxed way of doing a board presentation to go down well. But make no mistake; this is not an off the cuff meeting, far from it.

Military planning

Back at the office you have already had a run through on what you are going to say. You have covered all the points that you are going to discuss. You have worked out the timings of when your team will come in and deliver their part of the presentation, and what they are going to say. You have checked out the agenda with your coach and decided that the SVP of sales will front all questions and then palm them off to the team if he or she can't handle the question.

Run your presentation past others – stress test it. Too often we are in our comfort zone, talking our language. *See things* from the perspective of the prospect.

> What appears to be a seemingly 'off the cuff' meeting for the prospect actually needs to be extremely well prepared.

The 15 minute product overview

Sometimes the board presentation is simply a quick 15 minutes with the CEO alone. This can happen if the CEO has not been involved in the detailed evaluation and just wants a 30,000 feet overview from the vendor. They are not interested in the detail but will want to meet the people that are about to sell them some software or service.

On the tee

We once sold to a famous company where a very well known business personality was the CEO. The CEO had heard all about OneWorld (E1) and wanted to get an overview of the product. We had won this deal so all we had to do was to go into the boardroom and offer a 15 minute overview of the software. So this was a product demo and luckily for me my background is accountancy. I did not want our presales person to do this demo as it needed to be really slick, so it was me and Mike (my sales guy) that went in.

Now I had never met the CEO but she had a powerful reputation and had been described as the 'most powerful blonde in business', so I was a bit nervous. We set up in the boardroom. I had practiced the 15 minute demo and was ready for anything. Except what happened next.

In walked a drop dead gorgeous blonde woman. She went straight to a swivel chair that was next to us and said "I have heard good things about OneWorld. Impress me." She then tucked her legs up onto the swivel chair, did a 360° spin in the chair, and stared at me waiting for the demo of a lifetime.

I started the presentation but all the things I was going to show just vanished from my brain. I was pitching to a beautiful, highly intelligent, no nonsense woman who had thrown me with her unexpected chair swivel. I was working on auto pilot not really knowing what I was doing. I started to do a "Gardening Glove" demo…

> A Gardening Glove demo was a term we used when one of our presales people did a really bad demo. In effect it's like trying to type on a keyboard with oversized gardening gloves on - you just keep hitting the wrong key all the time.

Back at the presentation - my sales guy was looking on in horror but my training took over.

- Never apologize.
- Always look confident.
- Just plough on.

After some 10 minutes the CEO said that she had seen enough and walked out. No apology from our end, we just looked confident, and our coach showed us out.

Mike and I got into the lift. Not a word was said. I waited until we left the building and said: "Sorry about that. I sort of screwed it up a bit."

"A bit? S*** that was terrible Nick," replied Mike. "It was like a bad magic trick that kept going wrong. Like the ones at kids' parties where the magician keeps saying *is this your card?* and all the kids shout out NO and then you select another one that is wrong again."

"Well what would you have done?" was my reply.

We both burst out laughing as Mike understood how I got thrown off course. The only thing for certain was that we would never get another opportunity to impress the CEO as much as we did then, "NOT".

The CEO must have left the meeting feeling that she probably did not understand this very technical product as my presentation was nothing but completely baffling. However, if one of the leading consultancy firms and all her management team wanted it, then it must be good, and it just must have been a bit over her head.

The power of *saying nothing* had worked. We had not apologized for a poor demo and had not confirmed any doubt in the prospect's mind that the demo was terrible. Anyway I must not have done too much damage as they bought the software.

Setting you up for hole 17 - "Negotiation"

More and more buyers are getting schooled in the art of negotiation. It's not just sales people that go on courses but professional buyers and managers now know the tricks as well, although they should not be anywhere near as good as the professional sales rep.

Sometimes two vendors will be asked to do a board pitch, keeping both in the game even though the buyers have a preferred solution, so that they can negotiate a better price. Also your coach may now fear losing his or her job if they give you any information that will tell you just how well you are doing because this will reduce the prospects negotiating position.

Just be aware of this but remember - *you are the professional in sales and negotiation not the prospect*. By now with the reference visit under your belt where your existing customer has told you that the prospect 'wants to buy', and a good board presentation out of the way, you know you hold a number of aces ready.

Summary

Most board presentations will not be made to the very top "C" level people. You need to make sure that the final high level pitch is done to "The Right Level" not necessarily "C" level.

Keep the presentation high level and relaxed, and leave people with three things to remember (i.e. the three reasons to buy your software or service). Don't get confrontational or you will lose. Be prepared to get 'set up' for the negotiating phase by the prospect keeping two suppliers in the game.

We are now ready to play the shortest hole on the course, the 16th. This is the point of no return when the decision is made. Once made there is nothing that can be done about changing the prospect's mind if you want to remain a credible vendor in the market place.

The 16th hole
Decision Time

There is a time in every deal where there is basically nothing you can do but wait for the decision. It's like Apollo 13 when they re-entered the atmosphere, five minutes of radio silence was like an eternity before we knew they were safe. Then again (and a little less dramatically) it is similar to times when you have just finished your round and all you can do is wait to see if anyone else comes in with a better score. We have reached the *point of no return.*

On this hole

- When all goes quiet.
- The point of no return.
- Nothing you can do?
- Sales strategies for losing.

When all goes quiet

This is it. The decision is being made. There will now be two to three days of loss of contact with your prospect; you have no valid purchasing reason to call them and all you can do is wait for the verdict. The longer the call comes to say that you have won or lost - the less chance you have of winning.

The point of no return

Decision time is where your powers of persuasion and influence need to be halted as they won't help anymore. This is where you find yourself *just before* the decision is made. For the buying team, they have come down on the side of one solution over another, and the Empathy Selling "P's" in the buying team are trying to make sure they get what they want.

Before the decision you had the chance to lower your price, or make a commitment on a modification or a service that the prospect needed. But once the wheels of judgement are in motion there is nothing that you can say, or do, that will change the prospect's mind.

Nothing you can do?

The wait is the worst part of any sales cycle as you sit there and twiddle your thumbs. You have completed the sales process, and done your best, implemented the right strategy, cultivated all the right people and you have a product fit that's great. So you should just relax and wait for the call that you have won the deal.

I look back on all the deals I have won and it's never like this, no matter how good a sales campaign you have run. As you wait, your coach will have been told *not* to talk to you. You have put your best price forward; but you just don't know what is going to happen. Of course, when the deal comes in, it's easy (after the event) to say: "we had this in the bag all the time," but if you ever think like that - you will lose.

On the tee

Before implementing a sales process in the late 1980s I was having a chat with an account manager from IBM. We had been bidding on a client of his and he rung me up to tell me that we had lost the deal. I immediately called in the sales rep of the account and asked how he was doing on this account. Calmly he said: "No problem Nick, we should close this in a couple of week's time."

The problem with this rep was that he was so overconfident on everything he did. He would not take any advice, and the combination of overconfidence and not taking advice meant that sales was not a career for him. Compare that attitude to the very best sales person I have ever worked with - even when he had been told that he had won the deal he was still working hard, and refused to accept the decision until the contract was signed.

I always want a sales rep to have said: "I could have done more". Paranoia is a good thing for a sales rep, without acting paranoid around the prospect I might add, because it focuses your mind to do more. Remember the two rules:

1. Everyone lies to you
2. Always rely on being let down

Anyway, back to thumb twiddling time. You have forecasted this as a done deal, a best fit in fact, and now you wait for the call.

Selling begins when your prospect says no!

Bad news. Let's pretend that the prospect has come back and said they will pass on your solution. You may think that this is when the selling really begins, and I totally agree with this when you are at holes 1 to 15. But *not* when you leave the 16th with a NO.

A number of sales people might argue with me here but any more selling will lead to animosity, loss of sales margin and the potential burning of relationships that you have made during the sales cycle.

Of course when you get the call that says you have lost the deal you can say that "I was only joking on the price and it really is X," to try to spoil your competitor's bid. But what type of vendor are you when the prospect has already asked for your best price? What else have you misrepresented in the sales cycle? Plus price is not really the deciding factor in most deals as you will see on hole 17th.

There are some schools of thought which suggest that if you are any good at selling you will be able to change their minds. Well, maybe, if you are selling Business to Consumer. But no way should you try this in a complex sale as it will be counter-productive. Remember the Empathy Selling saying "You can always tell a politician, but you can never tell a politician anything". Well the guys that have just made the decision are going to be "P's", they want their decision rolled out and, might I add, as quickly as possible

If you had not been able to sell to this prospect from all the earlier holes - what on earth makes you think that you can do this now? Sales companies might also try to wheel out bigger guns - "the owner of our company would like to meet with you to discuss the decision". What would the prospect say to that? "But why did we not meet him earlier, if we were that important to you?"

A 'belligerent' approach to bad news does not let you lose with grace and you might never get another chance to sell to this team of people, or more importantly get a really good debrief on why you lost.

How to lose with grace

I know I have covered part of this topic before but it's even more important to address this again on the 16th. To me once you get the call that you have lost, well, it's all over.

Lose with grace so that you can sell another time. Lose badly and your name will be mud. It's a small world and one day the sales rep that keeps on selling after a 'no' decision on this hole will run out of credibility over a lifetime of selling.

The losing strategy

Once you have accepted that you have lost this account then you need to have a formal loss plan in place; ready to be executed.

- Can you get a really good debrief on why you lost, to help with future sales?
- How can you keep close to this prospect in the future so that you can monitor the progress of how they are faring with your competition?
- Could you sell them your solution if things go wrong for your competition on this account?
- Can you sell them something totally different in the future?
- Can you sell to the people in the sales cycle if they join another company?

The debrief - who should do it and why?

Lost business is what every sales rep tries to hide, as covered on hole 3. It's a reflection on them as (if we are being particularly brutal) 6 months plus of work has achieved nothing. Actually that's not true. They have achieved something, they have cost the company money by engaging in a sale that either could not have been won at the outset, or where they have run a bad sales campaign. They have also given the competition the confidence to go into battle with you again. The winning competition will undoubtedly hold a debrief themselves on your product or services so that they will be even stronger the next time you compete with them.

Who should do it?

I feel that someone from the marketing department who is impartial should carry out the debrief and it should follow a set procedure. The best person should have Empathy Selling characteristics of Mover, Engineer and a high Normal. This profile means that they will get on with the ex-prospect, cover all the detail, and come across in a neutral manner.

Points to cover

- *People fit:* How did the sales team come across to the prospect, and were there any issues or clashes during the sales cycle?
- *Product fit:* In what areas did our product or services not fit your requirements and what could be done to improve them?
- *Company:* What was your feeling towards us as a company? Did you trust us and feel that we would be around for the long term?

- *Presentations:* Were they to the point and covered what you wanted based on your functionality? Or did we focus on our issues not yours?
- *User References:* What were your thoughts on the reference visits?
- Can we keep you on our mailing list and update you with new product releases?
- What were the key reasons why the competition won? (Product enhancements?)
- When was your internal decision made (i.e. should we have bailed out at a much earlier stage)?
- Did the people from the competition really impress you? (Maybe we should recruit them!)
- What could we have done better?

Now you can possibly see why sales reps and management would not want an independent person going in to discover this type of information, but just think what value this will be to your company. Feedback is important. Criticism, although it hurts, makes you a much better person in the future.

If you work for a supportive company then when they get this feedback they will work with you on it, and that's great. They are investing in you. If, on the other hand, you think you are simply moving closer to redundancy - you can see why sales people bury lost business.

What do you think the prospect will think of you as a company if you conduct a polished debriefing? They will probably view you as professional right down to the last and a vendor that should be respected. What information do you think you will be able to get out of them to help you improve? Vital information that will help you beat your competitor in the future.

And where should all this vital information be stored? Yes, in your CRM system under *lost business* with all the notes and recommendations attached and available for the rest of the sales force to see. Imagine having all this information to hand today… you might be working on a similar deal that is equally likely to turn out negatively. Perhaps you could have walked from this deal way back down the course?

> Make sure that you 'sell' a debrief to the prospect after you have been told a NO. That's the only thing that should be on the sales person's mind. This is the ideal time to get the prospect's buy-in to do this as they will probably be feeling very sorry for you.

You get a call from your coach with the bad news. "Thanks for the call, Geoff. I am obviously really disappointed but totally respect your decision," you say. "Can you please do me one last favour? Is it possible for one of my marketing team to come down in a couple of weeks and get a debrief on why we lost? We would really appreciate this as it will be of great help to us in the future. They could even do this over lunch if that is okay."

As we discussed on hole 3, lost business should be part of every sales management and board meeting as it is a most vital piece of information. I can confidently predict very few companies have a loss protocol in place because the sales rep and the management team just don't want to admit that they got it wrong in the sales cycle.

Taking the pressure off

I learnt very early in my sales career that reporting bad news early meant that something could be done about it, and bad news reported late meant lost business. If you work for a company that delivers pressure from the top down then this pressure will end up back at the customer.

What I mean by this is that the CEO demands sales from the VP of sales who in turn puts pressure onto the sales management which ends up at the sales rep. "You had better close this deal Joe, by next quarter, or you will be history," commands the sales manager. What's that going to do for Joe? Well he certainly is not about to say to his manager "I am so glad we had this little chat as I wanted to say to you that I think we are in trouble with this account and I need your help." No, off goes Joe and rings up his coach. Joe starts putting pressure on him to say when he thinks this deal will close, or that if the deal is not closed this quarter you will end up with a new sales rep.

Sound familiar? Well this is where great sales management comes in and the trick is to take the pressure off sales reps so that they will take the pressure off their prospects and start talking the truth about accounts. What this means is that the pressure stops at the management level.

Maybe if your manager reads a copy of this book it will help you to get on with selling without the constant fear of losing your job?

This section is for sales managers

You know your team, they are all on compensation plans that incentivize them to close business early; so let them do their job professionally. One of the hazards of being a sales rep is the fear of being fired for non performance. Now provided the team are doing all the right things (and hopefully following the tips in this book) then as a manager, there is some logic in taking any rap and protecting the team.

In effect the manager truly leads his or her troops, and would be the first person fired before they got to the sales reps. Believe me - when you have a sales team that knows this is their manager's attitude you get much better feedback, loyalty and in turn better sales results.

> If you develop a work environment where people are not constantly under the threat of getting fired - people will be much more willing to own up to mistakes early.

Now I know that sales is a results orientated profession, so I am not saying here that you can have a sales force selling nothing every month, far from it. Pushing for a close when you have won an account (when you get to the 17th hole) is different from trying to close something that you have not won yet! But what I am saying is that if you are working for a good company with a good product and are following Ace the Sale then taking undue pressure off the team will help you to close far more business and if business is not coming, then the company you are working for is probably at the end of its sell-by-date and it's time to move on!

Keeping close to a prospect after you have lost

One of the most important things you can do during the sales cycle is to ask, if appropriate, to connect with your prospect on LinkedIn. Firstly, as discussed before, this will be a good qualifier as to how you are doing because if the invitation is readily accepted then it's a good indication that you are doing well. Secondly if you lose the deal and you have lost with grace you will also have ongoing contact with the prospect. LinkedIn allows people to *stop* being connected to you and if you see this happen after a sale, you will then know that you have burnt your bridges for the future with this person.

Okay, you have successfully managed to sell the debrief meeting and your marketing person has done a great debrief with the prospect and has updated the CRM system with lots of details. The marketing person has also secured permission from the prospect to keep them on the mailing list so that they can receive future information and occasionally take the odd call to see how they are doing.

One thing that you must not do is start spamming this person every day with irrelevant information. These contacts need to be flagged up as lost business and contacted on a quarterly basis. "Old is Gold" was a famous saying in my selling days as - many times - an old prospect could become a gold bar as things changed from the prospect's position. There might be a change of management, a management buy-out, or the bought in solution just did not hack it and the prospect is back on the market again.

On the tee

We had been working a US multinational account based in New York and we were then selling to the UK division of the account. We had a product issue because the CEO in the UK wanted us to deliver reports in exactly the same format as he had on his desk that day. We could deliver better management information but not in 'exactly the same' format.

Our US based sales rep made contact with company HQ and built a good relationship with the CIO and explained the situation. We lost the deal because we could not deliver the report in exactly the format the prospect wanted, and so they bought another product. One that was claimed could do everything.

Just a little quote from a buyer friend of mine who bought a lot of software and capital equipment: "The product that can do everything from day one ends up doing nothing forever." How right he was in this case.

We lost with grace and kept in contact with the US CIO. She said that she wanted the UK to make their own decision but recognised that we could deliver the numbers but not in the format they wanted.

Six months later when my US sales guy made a call to her - we were back in the game. The supplier that won could not deliver on the numbers, the UK CEO had left and she was now taking charge of the reporting project. Three months later we signed a worldwide deal with them.

Now what a coup this was. Our competitor who had won this deal had been kicked off this account and we had a really good customer who would willingly share their experience with our future prospects. One more competitor was eliminated because we kept close to lost business. "Old is Gold".

> A prospect that you lost to a competitor, but then win back later, is worth so much to you when you compete with them again. "Just talk to XYZ Ltd," you say to your coach. "They bought our competitor's product and threw it out after 6 months. Please feel free to give them a call."

Management change

Another occasion, when maintaining a relationship worked, was when we were trying to sell to a large oil company. At the time the people in charge did not select our software but we kept in contact as we had avoided burning any bridges. Over time people changed and we quietly tracked these changes in our CRM system. Eventually new management appeared and we were able to sell a multimillion dollar deal to them three years after we were first rejected.

Can you sell them something different?

As we discussed back on hole 4, building a sandwich type product (a low cost entry solution) can get you into an account under the radar of the board so that you can up sell later. At The GL Company there were customers who just did not want to buy our software as they already had Business Intelligence tools that they thought could do the job. We continued to keep good relationships with these people though.

After I retired from GL I kept in close contact and years later the company came up with a brand new product that reconciled key control accounts and sold it on a rental model. They have now got into accounts that previously did not want their solutions and have sold successfully on the back of this new product. This is why you saw the big ERP companies buying up all the BI vendors in the mid 2000s as they were acquiring something different which they could sell to companies who had previously rejected them, giving access to the account again.

Selling to people that join another company

During the sales cycle you will have built up great bonds with some people, people that like you and trust your company. If they leave and are involved in another evaluation with your company it will be like meeting a long lost friend. However if you have burned all your relationships in a fruitless effort to win something that can't be won (when you get a NO) these people will often go out of their way to remove you from any future shortlists.

Summary

If you get a NO on hole 16th - it's the point of no return. Accept it and lose with grace. Having accepted the decision, get a great debrief on why you lost the deal so you are stronger the next time you meet this competitor.

Put a *losing strategy* in place, with CRM tracking, so that you can keep close to the customer and even make a sale in the future.

"Old is Gold" is a saying to remember. Keep good relationships with old prospects as things will change in time and they may become a live prospect once again.

Hopefully for us, when we get to the 16th losing will not happen very often, especially if you have read this book. So let's now suppose we got the *YES* we knew was coming, and let's play the signature hole, the 17th - *Negotiation*.

The **17** th hole

The Negotiation

You get the call and it is good news; but now the prospect wants to negotiate again. "Nick, we want to go with your company," says your prospect, "but we have an issue on price and some additional clauses for the contract. Can you come in and have a chat about all this?"

We are now about to play the best hole on the course: negotiation! It's a game that both sides want to win.

On this hole

- Negotiation is a game in itself.
- Negotiation chips.
- What's on the table.
- Different types of negotiations.
- How to give a discount.
- Why EQ is so important when negotiating.

Negotiation is a game in itself!

Negotiation is a game. I really want to make this point early on. You have been selected but (apparently) there is now an issue on price. Well after going through the process of selecting your company, price is seldom the reason why someone won't buy. What they want is to negotiate a bit more discount before they sign the contract. They want to play.

All companies play the game differently so this hole has a lot to it. You can get the nice negotiation which is done over a cup of coffee, right down to the professional team who are there to negotiate the very best deal for the company. Some companies will take two vendors through to the 17th hole, but unless they tell you that you are the preferred vendor why discount anymore? You have already submitted your best price and they have made their decision, so normally the 17th hole has no competition on it.

Before you go into any negotiation you need to have your negotiation chips lined up.

Negotiation Chips

Negotiation chips are things that you can 'move on' in the negotiation, and here is a typical list in a software sale.

- Clauses in the contract that you can live without. This is where any clauses that you put into the contract, on the 11th hole, can be removed.
- Other clauses in the contract that you can negotiate on. This is when you change certain wordings to reflect the prospect's requirements (and you are happy to live with the changes).
- Payment Terms. Starting off with the very aggressive payment terms that you put in place on hole 11 - you now have room for negotiation.
- Discount on software. You have given your best and final offer but the prospect just wants to have another go for fun.
- Discount on maintenance. A real 'no no' here in software sales but you could be a little bit flexible if need be.
- Discount on services. Again services should not be negotiated on, but if the prospect was willing to pay for 50 days upfront there may be a concession.
- Availability of implementation staff. Now that the prospect wants to become a customer they will want to move quickly. Committing to an installation plan will help smooth the way on other issues.
- Client testimonials. Again this is one of the clauses that we put in place on hole 11 that would be good to keep it if possible... but a good chip to have up your sleeve if you need to give it away.
- Additional functionality and timescales. During the sales cycle you might have identified some modifications that the customer needs.
- Future discount. This is really important. Always ring fence any discounts to your local territory and make them run out after say 1 year. Let them negotiate you up to 2 years.
- Member of the user group. Another good clause in the contract that you can take out if needed.

- Fixed price versus time and materials. Costing(s) should normally be done on a time and materials basis but the customer might want to negotiate on fixed price and fixed timescales.
- Reciprocal trading. If your customer has a product that you can use then agree to buy this instead of what their competition offers. Provided it makes commercial sense and doesn't breach any regulations.
- No bid. If you are really getting nowhere in the negotiation and get stuck on a show stopper. 'Walking' is a great call which, if done correctly, will normally succeed in bringing prospects back to your way of thinking.

The prospect will also have their own chips and you need to try to work these out before you go into any negotiation with them. Customer chips are mostly similar to yours but the other way around.

What's on the table

The most important rule in negotiating any deal is to recognise that there is only a certain amount of money on the table from the prospect. The trick is to get as much of this as possible without leaving too much behind. Companies will value your products and services differently according to their size and ego. Sometimes the money might be more than you think.

On the tee

A friend of mine ran an executive golf events company back in the 1980s when golf days were just starting up. The great thing about this type of business is that you end up dealing with the CEOs/CIOs of companies because they are really interested in getting involved. They love golf and want to know all the details. "What pros are playing? Can we go to the Belfry, and if not, is Turnberry available?"

Anyway my friend went in to see one of the most successful CEOs at a big company in the UK at the time. He was a raging Empathy Selling Politician with a capital P. "Sit down now. Tell me about this golf event," said the CEO.

After a few minutes he stopped my friend dead and said: "That's fine. I want it. What's the cost?" Well the normal price for this event was £20,000 but my friend has great EQ and just knew that this guy had an ego as big as they come, so he said "£40,000".

"Done!" was the reply.

My friend had negotiated a great deal based on the prospect and knowing exactly how much money was on the table (thanks to a very wealthy company with a CEO that had an ego to match).

The different types of negotiation

There are many different ways people play this game, and the one I like the best is the friendly negotiation. Let me explain.

On the tee

We were selling to a multinational engineering company in Stockholm and I got on really well with the CIO. It was one of those relationships where you start to become good friends. It was getting late and I was in the CIO's office with the contract. All the terms had been agreed but he was having one more go on price. The deal was worth about $400k and I did not want to go any lower.

"Roland, you know that you've got a great deal," I said. "Come on. Why don't you just sign it now and we can go for dinner?"

"But Nick," he replied, "I really think you should do this deal for $350. We are a big name and it will be good for your company."

This went on for a few minutes and then I said: "Roland I have a wife, three children and a mortgage to pay." I slowly took out my wallet and started to open it to show him the pictures.

Roland responded like he was in a gun fight at the O.K. Corral, and pulled out his wallet swiftly. "And so have I," he countered.

"Come on Roland," I sighed, "what do I have to do to get this deal signed at $400 tonight?" Roland thought for a moment and said: "Nick if you were to go down on your hands and knees and say please Mr Roland Jensen can I have this deal for $400k, then I will sign."

I thought for a moment and recalled a saying that a sales rep that worked for me used to say. *Never confuse pride with making money.*

"Okay," I said. "But you need to promise me one thing."

"What's that?" asked Roland.

"You must never tell anyone about what I am about to do. On your kid's life."

"Okay." He was smiling.

So down I went onto my knees, and said: "Dear Mr Roland Jensen please can I have this deal for $400k."

"Of course," he answered.

Roland signed the deal and off we went for dinner where we consumed a fair number of schnapps. Don't anyone tell you that negotiation is not a game!

The one way negotiation

On another occasion, we had already sold to a very big construction company and again had managed to get a first rate relationship with the CIO. He was yet another full on Empathy Selling Politician (they are everywhere!) so you couldn't argue with him.

We were about to do an $800k deal but all of this was for a new product that we wanted to develop. We had approached the customer to become the sponsor of this new software and the benefit to our business was huge if we could get this development funded (which the CIO knew).

After we did the board pitch and the sales guy sent off the pricing we heard nothing for a week. So he made contact and the CIO said we were too expensive. We then received a text message with just one number on it. *$600k.*

Now my sales colleague wanted to negotiate this up but knowing the CIO well I figured this would have pissed him off, and to be honest this was a fair price for what the up sell market opportunity was. However if we got back to him straight away it's likely we would have got a text saying '$500k'. So we needed to play his game.

"Let's string this out a bit," I said. "Text him back in a day's time with a polite note and ask if he can do the deal for $750."

The text was sent.

We got a text back almost immediately. *$600k.* That's all it said.

"Have another go tomorrow at $700," I advised.

We heard nothing for two days and my sales guy was starting to get worried. He tried in vain to contact the CIO but he had gone quiet on us so I emailed him and got a text message. *$600k. Take it or leave it.*

So we had clearly hit the CIO's threshold and now was the time to say thanks Mr CIO we really appreciate your support - please sign and return the new addendum. Which we did. We got a great deal that enabled us to up sell this new module to a number of our existing customers.

I call this negotiation "Text Ping Pong" and I am sure the CIO had fun with us.

> Never agree a price too early, even if you are happy with it. The prospect will think they could have done better, and may become resentful. You want this relationship to prosper in the future, so everyone needs to think they have done well.

The professional negotiating team

I have only witnessed this once in my negotiating experience. It took me by surprise but I would certainly be ready for it if I had to deal with it again.

On the tee

We were doing a deal up in Scotland and I had gone up the day before with my sales colleague. We had sampled some fine Scottish whisky the night before but we were not too worried. We thought this was going to be a 30 minute job and then we would head back home. How wrong we were.

We arrived promptly at 9.00am with a bit of a hangover and we were kept waiting for around 20 minutes. Eventually we were led into a very large room where the CFO (who we knew) was seated and two other people that we had never met were also waiting for us. I greeted the CFO. "Hello Michelle. Good to see you again."

"Hi Nick, please sit down. We want to go through a few things with you," was her curt reply.

The game was afoot.

"Right," began Michelle, "we don't like clause 3.2. Can we have that removed?"

"3.2? Yes that's okay," I said.

As she spoke, the person on her left hand side was just staring at me trying to read my body language as we discussed the various issues, it was really off putting. The other guy sitting on her right was furiously taking notes.

On it went.

"Yes, Yes, and Yes." I kept on agreeing with what she wanted. My headache just got a lot worse.

Michelle turned to the note taker, "can you please tell me where we are up to?" she asked.

"Yes Michelle. We have agreed the following 10 issues." He started go to through them.

Great I thought, we will be out of here soon. But no, off went Michelle again wanting more and more. We were on a roll of saying yes, and all I wanted to do was to get out of this most uncomfortable situation as soon as possible. I am a people person and this was like negotiating with a load of robots, there was no feeling or emotion present; just facts and figures with more and more issues that Michelle wanted.

We agreed the deal and I said we would send up an amended version of the contract the next day. But, to be honest, I had lost interest in this account. *How can you spend six months with us and build up all these relationships and then treat us like this?* I thought. *Thanks Michelle, you have got what you wanted but if anything goes wrong with your installation you will be the last company that I worry about.*

What had happened here is that these guys had been on a negotiation course. I call this type of negotiation the professional team negotiators. It will comprise of a spokesperson (i.e. Michelle who leads the negotiation), an observer to watch over events and act as an extra witness, plus a summariser who takes notes.

If you ever encounter this type of negotiating team it's not going to be fun and you need to use the following strategy. This is what should have happened…

Firstly make sure all options are on the table first. "Michelle before I can consider this request, are there any other issues that you have with the contract?" I would say.

"Yes Nick, we do have a number."

"Okay, then if you would please list them all out, I am prepared to consider them."

You then get your colleague to make notes on these requests so that you are matching the summariser and have your own copy of notes of the meeting.

Never give anything away without receiving something in return. "Michelle I am prepared to consider points 2, 3, 5 and 7, but in return I would want you to drop points 1, 4 and 6."

"Okay."

"Then we agree we are only going to discuss 2, 3, 5 and 7."

The negotiation continues on an 'I am prepared to consider your request in exchange for something else' basis.

You will hopefully not experience this type of negotiation too often. With the Scottish negotiation, the reason why things unfolded as they did (just being battered with point after point) was because the CFO had achieved a particular status in her company as she had a big ego. To satisfy her ego she needed to demonstrate to the world at large that she had power. Power over the vendor. Power over her employees. She was the main person at the meeting. Her profile was an Empathy Selling P, E, D that is Politician, Engineer and Double Checker. She had zero people skills.

In hindsight, I should have sent up my chief accountant to negotiate this deal. Despite my jibes earlier in the book, I do not belittle accountants. They do a great job. I was one for a while. Knowing him it would have been fun as both of them would have been at this negotiation for a couple of weeks getting nowhere.

The buying department

The 'buying department' is another problem negotiation as there are similar issues to the professional negotiation team. There are egos at play and the people you are negotiating with are completely removed from the emotional sales cycle that you have been going through over the last six to nine months. My first reaction is *Oh S***, this is going to slow the deal down.* One of the best strategies, therefore, is to get them removed from the negotiating team.

On the tee

We were dealing with a multinational pharmaceutical company and we had successfully sold our software to the European CFO. I got a call from my coach "Nick, great news. We want to go with you, but the bad news is that our buying department wants to get involved. I just want to warn you they are a bit tough."

After two weeks of trying to track down the main buyer I got this email:

> Nick, I am tied up and can't get to your deal until next month. In the meantime here is a copy of our contract that we would like to go with.

The contract was totally unacceptable so I called up my coach and said that unfortunately we couldn't do business. Considering the prospect had been reconciling the fixed assets in excel to the wrong files in their ERP system (which our software discovered) and could not reconcile the Business Intelligence system to the ERP database (which our software did in a matter of minutes) I thought I was in a pretty strong position.

Bingo. The buying department was removed, we won the deal and I got an apology from the CFO.

Now there are many times when you can't make this happen so you need to go through the process, keeping your coach in the loop all the time. "Eric, we just had a meeting with your buyer and he is insisting on a change to the liability clause. Can you please get him off our backs as this is a deal killer for us," you say; and Eric helps you out.

The legal negotiation

Another tough one, and one that is sure to extend the close by a couple of months, especially if they use an external lawyer.

You have agreed the price and payment terms but you have just got a copy of the contract back from the external lawyer with so many changes to it that it's now looking like a rewrite. The problem here is that things will get sorted out but it's going to take time, time that you don't have as the quarter end is approaching fast.

If you have an internal lawyer in your company and you are great at internal politics then your contract is going to get sorted first. So just pass this over to them and let them argue over semantics. You will need to get your coach onboard again. The external lawyer from the prospect's side is being paid by the hour so the longer this goes on the better it is for billing. You can sometimes get away with saying: "you know the 7.5% discount we negotiated? I am afraid we can now only offer 5% because of the time this is going to take our lawyer to sort things out." This has worked in the past for me and the prospect's lawyer has been hurried along and forced to concentrate on the main issues.

These professional negotiations sort of spoil the fun a bit, so let's get back to negotiating with the main man.

He who speaks first loses

We were selling to a UK brewery and the chairman (Stephen) was an old family member of the brewery and a really nice guy. We got on well but it was a professional relationship and not one where we went down the pub as mates.

We wanted to charge for a modification which our IT Director was happy to discount but I was working with a new sales rep and I wanted to show him the ropes with negotiations. "Nick, Stephen is not going to be happy with this modification charge on top of the new software he is buying," said my sales guy.

"Ok let's go down there and negotiate this," I said. So off we went.

As we were waiting to go into the boardroom I said to my colleague: "there is going to be a pretty uncomfortable moment in this meeting and promise me that whatever you do - you don't say a word when this moment comes."

"Okay," was his reply.

We entered the room, and started to talk about the new software, and we agreed upon the price. Stephen then started to talk about the modification: "Nick, about these additional charges. Do we have to pay this much?"

It was a question that anyone with good "EQ" would have seen through. Stephen was happy to pay for the modification, but he was actually looking at whether I would discount it. If he had said: "Nick, you have really pissed me off about this additional charge. What do you think you are playing at?" - I think I might have made a different call. As it was, I motored on.

"Yes Stephen, that's the price." Then it went silent.

The silence was deafening (if you get what I mean). 10 seconds passed and we headed on to 20 seconds with no one talking. My sales rep's foot started to tap gently up and down. I dared not look at him in case he broke the silence.

21… 22… now you try keeping quiet for 22 seconds! Try it now, it's a long time.

23… 24… 25…

I just stared right at Stephen.

26… 27… 28…

"Okay Nick." He finally spoke. "That seems fair."

"Great, thanks Stephen. This modification is just want you need," I replied.

"I know," he said.

That was a long 30 seconds but was an important lesson in negotiating, and it was great fun.

How to give a discount

Offering discounts should always be given with caveats, conditions and complexity. In the same way that complex pricing is good for negotiation, complex discounts are good to protect your margin.

The straight percentage

Always use fractions of percentages when negotiating a percentage discount. If you give 5% the customer will want 10%. If you start off at 3.5% then you will get negotiated up but you have already set the bar. 0.5% of a percent is a big number for you.

Quantity discounts

Prospects will always try this on. "We are going to buy loads of your software. What we need is a 40% discount upfront."

One of the best deals I ever did was for a large battery company that had users throughout Europe. They wanted a big discount upfront. I invented the claw back discount schedule which got me into a bit of trouble back at the US HQ. They had never heard of it, and it was not in the price book.

I sat down with the prospect and said: "Okay, if you are going to buy all these users - show me where they are and over what timescale they will be employed."

"Right," replied the CIO, "we have 50 in the UK, 20 in France, 30 in…." and on it went.

I drew up a schedule with all the users and all the timescales that I was told, and we ended up with a big number minus a 40% discount.

I opened up the discussion. "What I will do is apply the 40% discount now to your 50 UK users, but if you don't buy another 100 in a year's time the discount will be clawed back to 20%. If the other 50 users do not come online in 2 years time, I want another 10% back."

"Okay," said the CIO confidently. He was over the moon that he had got his 40%.

Fast forward one year, and you can imagine his reaction when I pointed out that he had only bought 60 of the additional users. It nearly worked out cheaper for him to buy these additional 40 users than give me back the discount he had. That certainly was the case in year two!

Always put timescales on discounts. Never leave them open ended. It's something that prospects just don't see as they are focused on today. It protects the review for the company in the long run and helps protect your position in your company as a certain sale is going to happen later in the year.

Ring fence discounts

If you are doing a deal in the UK, keep it in the UK. Never mortgage someone else's revenue. I have done this so many times - "if you have this percentage discount Mr Prospect then it only applies to you, and no one else". This is fine as people only think of their own situation and don't care if another territory has to start over again, as there is nothing in it for them.

You could argue the same for the sales rep but just think how (when the whole sales force is doing this) a deal from the US drops into your territory and you are not lumbered with a 40% discount as a starting position. So it is in your interest to do this.

Any pricing proposal should have an expiry date attached to it, however small it is. This will help you to close the deal when you need to.

Playing snooker for $5000 per frame

Insight Database Systems (IDS) was sold to Hoskyns and there was a one year "earn out" for my boss to reach the acquisition price that had been agreed. When the Hoskyns deal went through - the manufacturing software we were selling at the time (developed by SSA) was pulled from under us, as SSA said that ownership had changed and our contract had been broken.

Off went the (now) former owner of IDS and promptly bought Data3 with his own money and signed a contract with Hoskyns to resell the software. Problem solved and I then left Hoskyns to work for Data3. This was an amazing deal as Hoskyns could not go back and buy Data3 for themselves as they thought they already had manufacturing software when they bought IDS as they had the agency agreement with SSA. If they went back to the board to ask for more money this would caused huge embarrassment as they were a public company.

Anyway the deal was this. When IDS was sold my boss got a payout of 50% of the software sales for the first year. There were other products that were 100% owned by IDS but as he now owned Data3 and was getting a 50% royalty from Hoskyns (he had signed them up as an agent) in effect he got 100% of any sale of Data3. Good deal, although my boss did have to buy out the UK distributor for a million pounds so that Hoskyns could then resell Data3.

We all knew that the idea was to build up Data3's sales and then flip it in a year's time, so to save costs - I was working out of the chairman's country house in the snooker room. Next to me was the product support guy and a secretary. So in the morning after making a few calls and writing some letters (no email then) I would turn around to my colleague and say "Fancy a game?" and that was it for the rest of the day. We did actually get very good at snooker.

Right, I will get back to my point, now that I have painted the scene. We had got to preferred supplier status for a UK PLC and they wanted a bit more discount. We could have just said "yes" but I knew that the CIO was a bit of a snooker fan and he knew we were working from the chairman's snooker room. So we suggested that we should play for $5,000 dollars a frame - 4 frames only and they could not lose anything. We were putting up a $20,000 additional discount if they won all the frames.

Needless to say we had a great afternoon and we did manage to get $5,000 dollars back but we were not really trying too hard. This game of snooker really cemented our relationship with the purchaser and it was even featured in Computer Weekly, which in those days was the only magazine worth reading about computers in business.

A year later Data3 was sold to ASK, so job done. It actually took ASK three months before they found out that we were working from a snooker room and they called me. "Nick, I believe that you now work for us," the HR director said. "Would you mind coming in and working from our Milton Keynes office?"

"No problem," I replied. "Do you have a snooker table?" I don't think the HR director got the joke.

Why EQ is so important in negotiating

There are hundreds of books available on how to negotiate but unless you go down the route of the robot negotiator, like in the professional negotiations, then EQ will play a small part in these types of negotiations.

"I will give you this if you will give me that" is not exactly difficult but you will end up in a long drawn out negotiation best fought out by two accountants. However, you could turn around and say: "you know what's going to happen once you have got this software up and running? You will start to sell more, reduce overheads, and increase customer satisfaction which to a multi-million dollar turnover company like yours is worth many millions of dollars. So our software is cheap in comparison, and the sooner you start the sooner you will see these benefits."

This approach focuses minds beautifully, but you are unlikely to find this deal tactic in many books. If any.

The best negotiators are people with the highest EQ. They need to be able to read people and situations, and leave very little on the table. If you want to negotiate well, go back to hole 2 and increase your EQ.

Picking up on what people are really thinking compared to what they are saying gets you higher value deals. I knew that the chairman of the brewery did not mind paying more for the modification. It was obvious from his tone of voice. I knew that we were about to really piss off the CIO of the building contractors who texted *$600k take it or leave it.* That is EQ in action.

Summary

Negotiation is a game so let people play. The professional negotiator can put a deal back a couple of months. Use your coach to get them removed or force them to become more flexible.

Be prepared to walk away from the deal once you have won it if the negotiations become too one sided. Normally common sense will prevail and you will end up agreeing.

There is only so much money on the table; it is the sales rep's job to find out exactly how much there is. Sales reps with a high EQ will be the best negotiators.

So we have now negotiated the deal but the contract is not signed and the money is not in. We are off to play the 18th - getting the contract signed.

The 18th hole
Contract Signature

So all the hard work is done. You are now on the last hole and things are going to be easy. All you have to do is to get the contract signed and the deposit paid. Well, that might not be as simple as you think.

What we will cover on this hole

- No urgency from the customer's point of view.
- Don't delay as things can change.
- Put a signing strategy in place.
- Forcing a close.

No urgency

We can finally call the prospect 'the customer', or can we? After six to nine months work you have finally got there, everyone is happy, the contract has been negotiated and the price is fine. You have achieved a win-win agreement but the customer, ahem prospect, seems to have no urgency in getting the contract signed. The evaluation team have done their job and selected the best vendor but there is no rush to sign the contract straight away. "We can do this in a month's time," your client tells you. "After all, the whole thing is going to take 18 months to implement anyway".

This attitude does not help you. One month in a sales cycle can mean missing your quarter number or worse still your yearly target. It's like being 4 up with 5 to play, you think you have it in the bag but if you don't close the game out as soon as you can - things can go horribly wrong.

On the tee

We were selling a CRM system to a company just outside London where the main driver of the project was the CIO. We had done a terrific job, won the deal and the contract was ready to be signed. It was Friday and we could have gone to pick it up but we were in no hurry - "we can get this signed next week, Monday will be okay to get the contract".

Tragedy struck. We called the CIO the following week and were advised that he had died over the weekend of a heart attack. We were told: "Your project? We don't know what is going to happen with everything he was working on. But call back in a couple of weeks as all the staff are in shock."

A few weeks later we tried to create some momentum but there was no one interested in pursuing matters. "We will look at it in a month's time," said the CFO, and this is how it went on until eventually it just faded away.

On the tee

Here is another one. After nine months work selling to a building manufacturer and winning the deal - the prospect was taken over by a bigger rival who used a totally different ERP system. Luckily for us we got the deal signed a few days before the announcement came but if we had dragged our feet this deal would have been stopped.

Now these are extreme examples but hopefully the sad story and the company takeover makes my point. If a contract is ready to sign *get it signed there and then*. Go down personally and pick it up. This is a good strategy because if someone says that they will sign today and you are actually sitting in reception the chances are that it will get signed. If, however, you are waiting for a fax or for them to post it, it's easy for something to come up at the office that distracts the signer's attention. What's more, the longer you don't have the contract the greater the chance that something bad might come along. Your competitor might have just signed a big order that they could not have discussed at the time of the sales cycle. Legislation might be announced that makes the solution redundant. Perhaps your main sponsor gets head hunted or fired. Get my point?

If a contract is ready to be signed go down and pick it up there and then.

So, if there is a lack of urgency in proceedings - what should you do next?

Put a signing strategy in place

You need to sit down with your coach or better still, because you are the vendor of choice, you can now speak directly to the economic buyer. You need to know what steps are in place to get the contract signed and the deposit paid. This would be a typical situation.

"Nick," says the economic buyer, "firstly we need to get board approval. Don't look so worried (she is high in EQ and just noticed the look of horror that has come across my face). It's just a rubber stamping exercise. But we must get this done before I can sign."

"When is the next board meeting?" I would say.

"The next one is at the end of the month."

"What about getting the cheque sorted out for the payment on order?"

"Oh we need to get a purchase order in the system as well," she adds. "Thanks for reminding me."

I have another question: "And who will sign the contract?"

"Oh that's me. But I think I might be on holiday the week after the board meeting. Let me check."

As you can see, there is a lot going on and you can understand why it is so important to have discounts linked to dates so that you can politely remind prospects that if the contract does not make the agenda at the next board meeting the cost of your project is about to rise significantly.

Now this process should have been unearthed way back down the course but it is easy to focus on trying to win the account rather than what happens when you win it. You want no surprises in the signing process. In your CRM system, under opportunities, you should have these fields filled in:

- Date of the board meeting for approval: MM/DD/YYYY.
- Is the person who is signing the contract in on this date: Yes/No.
- Who will raise the purchase order: Name of the person.
- Can you get payment on time: Yes/No.

All filled out way before the 18th hole!

Things that can go wrong

You can get the order with no payment, but it is useless as you can't book the deal. You can get the purchase order without the contract but, once again, this is useless. You can get the cheque without anything else.

You need to have a plan to know who is going to get all the above done, and by when. This is why you see so many deals slipping in sales forecasts - the sales rep is 'hoping' all this will happen. This is fine if the customer is desperate to start the project and they are pushing you harder than you are pushing them. But ask yourself this question - who needs this deal signed quicker, the customer who is going to take years to install your solution, or you who needs to close it this month to get to performance club?

Forcing a close

Back on the 16th, I mentioned that you can't force a close until you have won the account and are on the 17th and 18th. There will be times when prospects will drag their feet and show no urgency in signing the contract when you get to this hole. This is when you need to force a close.

On the tee

We were selling to a large pharmaceutical distributor in Finland and we were doing well. Finnish people are really interesting, and when they came over to the UK we took the whole team out for dinner.

There was not much conversation as the Finns are very serious but when we had finished the meal and moved onto coffees we asked them if they would like any liqueurs. Well that was a silly question because that's what they were all waiting for. "Oh yes please!" was the unanimous cry. "We would all like a brandy and another one, and another one!"

The evening was starting to come alive I don't know why we bothered with the meal. I reckon we should have got in a McDonalds order, and got down to the brandies a bit earlier.

The next day they were all in a good mood, did not ask too many questions on the demo, and wanted to leave early so that they could go duty free shopping on their way home.

> If you ever sell to a Finnish company make sure you have access to a lot of brandy.

Before long we had won the Finnish account and it was worth $2.7m in software sales and over $2m in services but we were working with another company - a systems integrator - as they were selling the hardware and additional services. Our deal had a drop down dead date of October which also was our year end. If we missed this deal we missed our number.

The systems integrator's year end was December and they wanted to roll everything onto their contract. I mentioned to the system integrator and the client a number of times that we needed this deal by October otherwise the software was going to cost $4.5m. However no one seemed to be taking much notice so we arranged a meeting in Finland with all the parties present. Our objective was simple: to get the deal signed before October 31st.

Rod (my sales rep colleague) and I entered the meeting room where the project team leaders were waiting, as was the system integrator's sales rep (Hugh). We got down to business pretty quickly and Hugh rolled through his agenda, thinking that we would just follow on and accept the delay in the deal.

"Excuse me," I interrupted, "you keep going on about a December close, but you know that our deal is dependent on our contract being signed in October." No one seemed to think that this was significant. I continued. "If you don't sign the deal, the cost goes up from $2.7 to $4.5m. All for the sake of 3 months."

This got the attention of Ulcar who was the project leader and executive sponsor from the prospect's side. We had a good relationship with him but I felt this was about to change. "This is outrageous," he said. "You can't do that Nick."

"Ulcar," I replied, (it's always worth starting off with someone's first name if you are about to tell them bad news) "the additional discount you negotiated was done on the understanding that we would get a signed contract by October 31st. I was able to negotiate this discount on the basis of this commitment. But I am afraid that if you don't sign, the additional discount is lost and we go back to the $4.5 number."

There was a deathly hush, no one talked, and the look on Ulcar's face was of someone who was about to commit murder.

"I am very displeased about this," he said.

We stared at each other.

"You know Nick we could always go back to the other vendor," threatened Ulcar.

"I know Ulcar," I replied, still using his first name. I wanted to add: "that is a chance that I will just have to take," but my EQ thought better of it.

Then it went quiet.

Remembering that *the first person who speaks loses*, Rod and I said nothing. After what seemed an age, Ulcar piped up again. "Okay, we want to discuss what to do next with the team. Please leave the room and wait at reception."

Off we went, like two kids who have just got into trouble at school, and been told to wait outside the headmaster's office.

Rod was starting to look a bit pale, his whole year was dependent upon this deal whereas the SUMA region would still be close to our number. He had everything to lose. We took the long walk down the corridor back to reception and sat down, Rod started to talk. "Are you sure you know what you are doing Nick?" he asked nervously.

"Trust me. We will be okay," I reassured him.

Poor Rod. There was I - playing roulette with his money. I think if it was his call he would have accepted a December close as his commission had been earmarked for a new extension on his house.

I explained my position. "This deal will just drag on as there is no guarantee the system integrator is going to get this closed in December. We don't want to be tied up in all their legal stuff. By the time this deal closes your territory would probably have changed and someone else will pick up the commission."

This seemed to have a calming effect but we did not talk too much after that exchange. You could feel the tension in the air. About 20 minutes passed and we were called back into the meeting room. We had no idea what was going to happen. All the work that we had done could just be blown away, but inwardly I was confident. We had a number of aces.

Ulcar informed us of the decision. "Nick, we don't like the way you do business but we are willing to sign your contract before October."

"Thank you Ulcar. You have all the paperwork and we will begin work on getting this out of the way so that we can start on making your implementation a success!"

There was no point in going into any more detail but I wanted to leave on a positive note. We just left the meeting and got out of the building as quickly as we could. The colour had just come back in Rod's face.

"Well done Nick," he said.

"No problem Rod. Just make sure you get that contract in by next week," I replied.

There is a point in all sales where you have to move from being the prospect's best friend to being assertive. I don't like this part of the sales cycle but it is a fact of life when you are in this business and unless you can do this - a deal will drag on and on with a real danger that you could lose it all together.

Oh, and by the way, I knew from my coach that the other vendor had pissed off the project team. When they went to see them, the VP of sales said: "You lot are a funny bunch. You don't say much. I would hate to play poker against you." That did not go down too well.

Forcing a close can only be done on the 17th and 18th holes when you have won the deal. This is why I say you can't use this play until you have won the deal because if you are still in a competitive situation you have no leverage.

With the Finnish deal above, it transpired that the system integrator's deal did not get signed until March the following year. We had to make hardware available for the customer to start the implementation, but we had our contract and payment 6 months before the customer had any of their own hardware to run it on. All ended well and we quickly moved on from this awkward situation to becoming best friends again. "Anyone for a Brandy?"

"Yes I think I will have one," said Ulcar.

When you have successfully negotiated a deal it may take several months before the deal is closed. This is the time to put pressure on your prospect to close, not before.

Summary

If you can get a deal closed today get it closed today or things might have changed by tomorrow. Go down and wait in reception if someone says they will sign your contract. What is one afternoon or a morning's work compared to a 9 month sales cycle?

Make sure that you have a closing strategy worked out and entered in the CRM system.

The ball is in the hole, and we have come to the end of the game. You've played 18 holes and won. You have a signed contract, a cheque in your hand, and you can now throw this all over the fence to the customer support manager to implement. You and your team deserve to go down to the 19th once again for a well deserved celebration!

The 19th hole (again)

The Clubhouse Revisited

Selling is a very emotional profession with many highs and lows. Being married to a sales person, especially if you are not from a sales background, is hard; one minute you are having the extension to your house you always wanted, the next week you have to sell the place as the deal you thought you were going to win has just gone south.

So when you get a deal - it needs to be celebrated and celebrated hard. Also you are only as good as your last sale so enjoy every brief moment. By closing a particular deal you have no prospects anymore!

But before the celebrations commence - do remember the internal politics. You did not win this deal on your own. There are many people to thank from the presales team to Patty on reception who made everyone feel welcome. An email needs to be sent out announcing your great win and mentioning everyone who was involved.

There are so many funny stories that I wanted to share with you over my sales career that just did not fit in when we were playing our round, but the 19th is a great time to tell them over a pint or two. Thanks for buying this book and getting this far. I really hope that it will make a difference to you. If you want to read on please do so but otherwise the very best of luck with your selling career.

Nick.

No software, no coffee and no loo paper

We were selling to a media company and it was going to be the very first sale in the world of our new open systems version of JD Edwards' OneWorld (now E1).

We were the preferred supplier on the deal because the CFO had just joined from a multinational music company that had our old AS/400 financial software installed worldwide (which he loved).

We had a final presentation with all the people that were going to use the software at our Stokenchurch office. There was one big problem, OneWorld had not really been written yet!

Back in 1997 when we were launching OneWorld we had a slight problem, the software did not work quite as expected so naturally we struggled to show anything at a demo. Coming off the back of great software on the AS/400 we had a fabulous reputation so people assumed that the new software would be just as good, if not better. We had just gone public and our CEO at the time had read "Crossing the Chasm" an interesting little read which was all about selling and not worrying about your customer. So we had to just sell and worry about the consequences later.

This was a period of time that I was not happy about which, as you read on the 10th, came back to haunt me when playing a game of golf in our winter league at my golf club. Some of the meetings I had to attend during this launch period would fill another book. Maybe another day…

Anyway the evaluation team all piled in to the office late one afternoon and because of the time of day there was no coffee or tea for anyone, *so no coffee*. When everyone was seated we had a problem, we could not show the OneWorld software as it was too flaky so we did the presentation on the old AS/400 software, so *no software.*

Then the economic buyer needed to go to the loo. Around that time we had employed a sales guy whom we affectionately called "Fat Davy". Now Fat Davy spent quite a lot of time in cubical one of the downstairs loo. Unfortunately the cubical that the buyer had gone into had no loo paper. Realising that there was someone in cubical one he asked if he could have some loo paper whereupon Fat Davy passed some sheets under the cubical to the thankful buyer, *no loo paper.*

Now having a man in cubical one had been quite an interesting strategy in the past. Many times Fat Davy would be in there when a prospect would enter excitedly talking to his colleague about the presentation and how they should buy our software, unaware that there was anyone in there. Fat Davy actually became one of our best sources of information for many a deal.

We won this deal, beat two very good open source suppliers to the account, and this deal became known as the *No Coffee, No Software and No Loo Paper* deal.

> Having someone permanently installed in cubical one of the toilets when demos are done can sometimes be your best source of information.

Customer Golf should you win or lose?

I was negotiating a deal with the CIO of the text ping pong deal (remember back on the 17th hole) and we were at an ERP conference in Las Vegas. We were trying to sell another $150k HR module but he was being difficult on price as per normal.

We had arranged to meet up to discuss the sale but he called me in my hotel room: "Nick," he said, "we are playing golf tomorrow at the Bali Hai Club. See you there at 2.00pm."

We went to the club house where I paid the green fee, bought a few balls (and a tee shirt for him) and off we went.

Well it was all very polite: "good shot," I said. "Nice putt." By the time we arrived on the 17th we were all square.

It was my honour and I thought - *Sod this*, I am going to beat this guy. I don't care about the $150k. I boomed the best drive of the day straight down the middle.

"Oh," remarked my customer, "so you are not playing *customer golf* any more then."

"No," I replied. "I want to win."

He boomed a drive down the 17th directly behind mine and off we strode down the fairway in total silence.

No putts were given and the concentration on both of our faces was plain to see. We halved the 17th and shook hands on the 18th after I holed a 15 foot putt for another half. "Nick that was the best two holes of non-customer golf I have ever played," he announced. "I will send you the contract in the post when I get back to the office."

> Always try to win at customer golf as the customer can always tell if you are not trying.

Roy Manuear and the Fish Interface

Back in the mid 80s when we were selling best of breed solutions, we were trying to interface the Data3 MRPII manufacturing solution to our financial systems. We had asked the product manager to come in and explain how this was going to work. Unfortunately for us he was an Empathy Selling Engineer, Double Checker and Artist.

After some 30 minutes of boring the sales team to death he started to draw the integration diagram on the flip chart. Well you would not believe it, there were lines and boxes *everywhere*. It was total madness and there was no way anyone in the room understood a thing that he was showing us.

When he had finished and left the room we all burst out laughing.

“I can’t believe how complex that was,” said James, who was one of the senior sales reps. “Now let me go through this again with you”.

James got up and started to scribble lines all over the flip chart like a man possessed and then he drew a big circle in the middle and said “This is a fish,” and he drew an eye and a tail. “And what we have here is the fish interface!”

From then on, whenever there was anything that was complicated, we called it *the fish interface!*

There is a point to my story. James came and joined me later at JD Edwards and he went out on a call to a big retailing client in Oxford Street. When he came back to the office he burst through my door. “Nick, you are not going to believe what I have just seen! There is a guy called Roy Manuear who has just shown me the most complex fish interface ever. He wants to integrate our software into his product management system. It was way over my head - you need to come along and see it.”

So off we go down to Oxford Street the next day for me to meet Roy and see for myself his really complex fish interface. James introduced me to Roy and said that I was more technical than him and he was sure that I would understand what he wanted. So Roy started to explain, and after about 10 minutes he said “Do you know what? I can show you on the flip chart exactly what I mean.”

As he walked up to the flip chart I started to smile to myself. Here is Roy Manuear with a name that sounds like shit just about to explain the most complex fish interface in history. Boxes appeared, lines were drawn, arrows rained down and sure enough the fish interface took shape. *What the hell are we doing trying to bid on this deal?* I thought. I dared not look at James as I was starting to feel my smile was going to change to a laugh so I stared straight ahead at Roy. Then all of a sudden I turned towards James and there he was - looking at me with an expression of *told you so - this guy is a madman*. James winked at me.

I can honestly say that this wink appeared to me as if it was in slow motion. It was like I was watching a film and the producer had slowed this bit down for added drama. By the time he had finished the wink I was in hysterics, uncontrollable laughter trying to disguise it as a cough. “Are you okay?” Roy asked me.

“Sorry Roy. I’ve got something stuck in my throat,” I coughed.

I could not stop myself and just carried on with this awful noise until I could not control myself anymore. I left the room saying that I was feeling a bit sick.

When I got to the office kitchen I just burst out laughing. It was like a drunk being sick, instead this time I was trying to hold back the laughter. Tears were rolling down my face and I thought how on earth could a professional sales person be laughing at a prospect like this?

I eventually calmed down. A big mistake. I went back to the meeting room as I thought that I was okay. But no, off I started again. I had to leave. This time when I left the room I left the building as well. James was on his own.

I waited outside for a while knowing I was going to get a bollocking from James when he came out, which I duly did. "Nick," James said. "Roy thought you were laughing at him but I managed to convince him that you had a problem with your throat."

"Good man, James." I replied. "Thank you but we won't be bidding on this deal anymore as I might die of laughter."

This was the first and only time this has ever happened but one day it just might happen to you. Try to think of the mortgage that you have to pay or all the money that you have borrowed to see if this stops you seeing the funny side of losing a deal.

Oh and by the way, when we filed the report about lost business it was due to the complexity of the interface not that we could not keep a straight face when we spoke to Mr Manuear.

Apple and Pears, Stairs

I was fortunate to work for a really talented guy in the mid 1980s who went on to become CEO of a number of well known software companies. I asked him if he had ever laughed in a demo.

"Laughed?" Bob replied. "How about total humiliation of a prospect!"

Bob was selling a worldwide deal to a Finnish company and the Finnish sales rep Bent was over for some sales training. Finnish people don't have a great sense of humour but Bent had potential and that night he went out with the sales team.

The sales team thought it would be a laugh to teach Bent a bit of cockney rhyming slang and here are a few translated phrases for you.

- Adam and Eve - for 'believe'.
- Ayrton Senna - for 'tenner'.
- Battle cruiser - for 'boozer'.
- Boat race - for 'face'.
- Chalfont St. Giles - meaning 'piles'.
- Dennis Law - for 'draw'.
- Family jewels - for 'balls'.

- Farmer Giles - for 'piles'.
- Hampstead Heath - for 'teeth'.
- Jimmy Riddle - for 'piddle'.
- Loaf (of bread) - for 'head'.
- North and south - for 'mouth'.
- Plates of meat - for 'feet'.
- Rosie Lee - for 'tea'.
- Sexton Blake - for 'fake'.
- Sweeny Todd - for 'The Flying Squad'.
- Trouble and strife - for 'wife'.
- Whistle and flute - for ‘suit’.

So off they go - talking rhyming slang to poor old Bent all evening until he got it.

The next day, Bent flies back home, and the sales team prepares for a telephone conference with one of the buyers of the Finnish company.

Roll on the conference call where the team (in London) led by Bob were in the meeting room as people started to dial in.

“Hi, Anna from Italy here.”

“Chris from Germany here.”

Then Bent called in. “Hi, Bent here. With Orson Kaart.”

Bob could not believe it. We have ‘converted Bent into a cockney’ he thought, and here he is taking the piss. “Orson Kaart” = Tart. That’s really funny.

So Bob just burst out laughing: “and I am the Dogs Bollocks!” was his reply. Everyone fell about laughing.

Unfortunately for Bob the laughter was so loud that he did not hear the pleas coming from the teleconference phone. “No Bob, No! It is Orson Kaart the purchasing manager.”

When the laugher died down and the mistake was identified the mute button was quickly pressed. At the London end, they had moved from something slightly funny to complete hysterics as all the team members began passing pictures of a tart to Bob as he tried to restart the conference call.

One of the guys was laughing so much he ended up underneath the boardroom table. The mute button was quickly pressed again as they tried to regain their composure. Needless to say that this was another lost deal.

Try not to laugh at your prospects. It just might harm your chance of closing the deal.

No that was a thirteen!

We were playing golf with a senior partner of one of the big consultancy firms at the Oxfordshire Golf Club which, if you have not played it, has a lot of water. I had invited my golfing buddy from JD Edwards along, and he was affectionately known as "Cash Point" as it was easier to get money out of him at golf than from an ATM machine. My children even used to send him Christmas cards addressed to dear Uncle Cash Point as most of their presents were funded by him every year.

Cash point was a single figure golfer and a real stickler for the rules. We got to the eighth where there is a dog leg right with water all the way down the right hand side. Our senior partner guest, who was responsible for a number of large deals, scuffed his drive off the tee and continued to have a nightmare on the hole. He put a number of balls in the water. I was feeling for him as this was meant to be a fun day out, and a 'thank you' for all the business he had introduced us to.

Anyway he eventually got onto the green and has three putts. Cash Point asked for the scores. "I was a five," says Cash Point.

"I was a four," I replied."

"I was a twelve," answered our guest.

Cash Point looked a bit puzzled and started counting to himself in his head. As we started to walk off the green we were called back. "No, that was not a twelve. That was a thirteen, let me go through your shots." And so he began: "1. knobbled off the tee, 2. in to the water, 3. penalty drop, 4. into the water…"

I could have died. Here was my best consultant being humiliated all over again. Thinking that he had already screwed up by taking a twelve was bad enough, but to relive every shot again and find out you took one more. Well I could just imagine what must have been going through his mind. "Oh yes, you are right, it was a thirteen," replied my once important senior partner of the big three consultants.

If the customer takes a twelve on a hole, it's a twelve! Move on quickly.

The Customer Support Manager

When I joined Insight Database Systems I was the customer support manager. I eventually moved into sales. I thought you might find this definition of the support manager (which was told to me by the international sales manager) amusing.

The customer support manager is a role within a software company where the CEO places a person between them and the problem, e.g. the customer. Normally when there is a new support manager the last one has just had a nervous breakdown and been moved on, or they have realized the enormity of the task in hand and changed careers just in time.

The new manager eagerly goes into the CEO's office and is presented with a shiny brand new white suit and a bucket. "What's this for?" asks the new recruit.
"Oh this is how I will know just how well you are doing," replies the CEO.

So off goes the manager with the shiny white suit on plus the empty bucket, and the phone rings. "Let me answer that," he says enthusiastically to one of his staff, "I want to get firsthand experience as to what is happening here." After some 30 minutes on the phone with 20 pages of issues the phone rings again, and again, and again. "You answer that one," he says to his assistant. It does not take the manager long to identify 30 action points on his to-do list on the first day. His bucket is starting to get full with the brown stuff. As time goes by the bucket starts to get full very quickly and the new manager is starting to have trouble catching all the muck that is being thrown his way.

His shiny white suit is now getting stained and the suit is starting to change colour, a light brown in fact. The CEO is not so keen to see him these days and the number of issues on the to-do list just keeps mounting up and increasing every day.

Eventually his suit has changed to a nasty dark brown colour. The CEO has just had an unhappy client directly on the phone to him bypassing the support manager who is now totally immersed with no more room on his suit to stop the issues hitting the CEO right in the eye.

This is when the CEO knows that the time is right for a new manager and the process of recruiting a new enthusiastic support manager starts again.

The Salesman

I want to leave the 19th with a joke that I am sure that most of you have heard but it's the best salesman joke I know, and is just right for the ERP sales rep in particular.

Eric Jones had been selling all his life and he had lied and cheated his way to numerous deals. Many a person he had sold software to had lost their jobs and split from their spouses due to the pressure of trying to get dodgy software to work. Their lives had been ruined by Eric who just carried on selling and having a great time.

One day he died and as he was standing outside the pearly gates waiting for St Peter to see him - he was thinking: 'I might be in a bit of trouble'.

St Peter came out with his big book. "Name?" he bellowed.

"Eric, Eric Jones," was the whimpered reply.

St Peter ran his finger down the book until he came to Eric's name. "Ah yes, are you Eric Jones, *the* Eric Jones who has lied and cheated and made other people's lives a total misery?" he asked.

"Yes I am," replied Eric. He did think about lying but even Eric knew that it was time for the truth for once.

"Oh this is interesting," said St Peter. "I have it down in my book that you have a choice between heaven and hell. I am instructed to show you both and then you can select where you want to spend eternity. Please follow me. We'll be using the lift."

This seems like a result thought Eric, and up he went in the lift to see what heaven was like.

As the doors opened there was calm music playing and people sitting on clouds in complete silence listening to the music. Eric waved at a couple of people he knew and then went back into the lift.

Down they went to hell and the doors opened. Eric could not believe his eyes. They were on a beach with beautiful woman everywhere. "Like a beer?" St Peter asked. Eric waved at David Rudd who was his Boss and much worse than him. He was water skiing and waving at Eric. How did he end up here Eric thought?

So back they went to the lift, returning to the pearly gates.

"Right Eric, you need to make your choice now," said St Peter.

"Well I know this is going to sound a bit silly," said Eric, "but I think I will choose hell."

"Okay," said St Peter, "I will just accompany you down there."

They rode the lift back down to hell, and as the doors opened St Peter pushed Eric out into this burning volcano. The Devil was coming towards Eric with a huge pitch fork with David Rudd's head on one of the prongs. Eric pleaded: "St Peter, St Peter, what happened to the beautiful girls, the water skiing and the beer?"

"Sorry Eric, but God said to tell you that that was just the demo!"

Appendices

The Empathy Selling Questionnaire

Complete the questionnaire and work out what type of character you are; circle one of the two statements in each box that is most like you.

Sometimes both options will feel like they are of similar weighting, so you will have to make a choice, and you need to circle the one that is *more/most* like you.

Once you have circled the appropriate statements in each box, you need to calculate your profile score by counting how many selected statements fall into each category. Use the bold number for the category.

e.g.

6. Creative, artistic and sensitive. (circled)
7. Will always ask for input, security minded

This counts as one statement in category 6.

Off you go!

6. Creative, artistic and sensitive. **7.** Will always ask for input, security minded	**1.** Like meeting new people and talking, always on the go. **2.** Conform and follow the rules. Concerned about what other people think of you.
2. Conform and follow the rules. Concerned about what other people think of you. **3.** Money motivated, always looking for a deal, can see an angle.	**4.** Never back down, always right. Want your own way. **1.** Like meeting new people and talking, always on the go.
4. Never back down, always right. Want your own way. **3.** Money motivated, always looking for a deal can see an angle.	**1.** Like meeting new people and talking, always on the go. **6.** Creative, artistic and sensitive.
3. Money motivated, always looking for a deal can see an angle. **1.** Like meeting new people and talking, always on the go.	**2.** Conform and follow the rules. Concerned about what other people think of you. **4.** Never back down, always right. Want your own way.
4. Never back down, always right. Want your own way. **6.** Creative, artistic and sensitive.	**2.** Conform and follow the rules. Concerned about what other people think of you. **6.** Creative, artistic and sensitive.
3. Money motivated, always looking for a deal can see an angle. **7.** Will always ask for input, security minded.	**4.** Never back down, always right. Want your own way. **5.** Project orientated and always completes things you start. Methodical.
1. Like meeting new people and talking, always on the go. **7.** Will always ask for input, security minded.	**7.** Will always ask for input, security minded. **5.** Project orientated and always completes things you start. Methodical.
5. Project orientated and always completes things you start. Methodical. **3.** Money motivated, always looking for a deal can see an angle.	**4.** Never back down, always right. Want your own way. **7.** Will always ask for input, security minded.

1. Like meeting new people and talking, always on the go. **5.** Project orientated and always completes things you start. Methodical.	**2.** Conform and follow the rules. Concerned about what other people think of you. **7.** Will always ask for input, security minded.
5. Project orientated and always completes things you start. Methodical. **6.** Creative, artistic and sensitive.	**3.** Money motivated, always looking for a deal can see an angle. **6.** Creative, artistic and sensitive.
2. Conform and follow the rules. Concerned about what other people think of you. **5.** Project orientated and always completes things you start. Methodical.	

Count up your scores

Trait	**1**	**2**	**3**	**4**	**5**	**6**	**7**	Total
Count								

Use the table above to count up your scores. Before you plot your results on the graph below, check that the total number adds up to 21 and the maximum number for any trait is 6.

For example:

Trait	**1**	**2**	**3**	**4**	**5**	**6**	**7**	Total
Count	6	2	6	4	0	2	1	21

Now plot your counts onto the graph below

Count							
6	-	-	-	-	-	-	-
5	-	-	-	-	-	-	-
4	-	-	-	-	-	-	-
3	-	-	-	-	-	-	-
2	-	-	-	-	-	-	-
1	-	-	-	-	-	-	-
	1	**2**	**3**	**4**	**5**	**6**	**7**
				Traits			

Now you can identify your traits:

1 = **Mover** the desire to communicate: (Extrovert)
2 = **Normal** the desire for social approval: (The balancing trait)
3 = **Hustler** the desire for material success: (Extrovert)
4 = **Politician** the desire to win: (Introvert)
5 = **Engineer** the desire to complete projects: (Introvert)
6 = **Artist** the desire to be creative: (Introvert)
7 = **Double Checker** the desire for security: (Extrovert)

A profile should be defined by the three highest traits, your balancing trait (which is *always* Normal), and your minor traits. In the above example it would be:

Dominant Traits	Balancing Trait	Minor Traits
Mover (6)	Normal (2)	Artist (2)
Hustler (6)		Double Checker (1)
Politician (4)		Engineer (0)

The above profile would make a good sales manager or VP of sales as the high Hustler component would make them able to look for angles in any deal. In turn, having 6 for Mover means that they will get on well with people and the Politician element will make sure that they get what they want in the sale and are focused to close business.

Good profiles for sales people will have dominant traits in Mover, Politician and Hustler (good for new business sales); and Mover, Politician and Engineer (installed based reps and new business).

Sample Large Account Strategy and Sales Splits

The objective of this large account strategy and sales splits document is to ensure cooperation between sales reps across countries and territories. Sales reps should not try to hide deals and sell into other people's territories. If this does happen then all commission will be taken away from the sales rep that closes a deal out of territory as the account rep has not adhered to this document. Working together will ensure that sales revenue is maximized not only for the rep but for the company.

Pricing

Local pricing should be based on the **Big Mac index**. The Big Mac Index is published by *The Economist* as an informal way of measuring the Purchasing Power Parity (PPP) between two currencies and provides a test of the extent to which market exchange rates result in goods costing the same in different countries.

So each local price needs to be calculated annually from the US dollar price list using this index.

Option 1. Single Country Pricing

If a deal is to be done that only affects a single country then it is down to the manager of that country to authorize any discounts and sales splits. NB - it is important that any signed contract ring fences the pricing and users of that location so that it does not impact upon another country in the future.

Even in a single country there might be occasions when a division of a company is evaluating software in one part of the country whilst company headquarters (HQ) are located in another salesperson's territory. Where appropriate this document can be used to resolve this issue.

Option 2. International pricing

This is the US price list plus 20%.

If a deal is to be done across multiple countries then international pricing must be used. Sales reps must explain to prospects the cost of doing business in multiple countries is higher than the target country that they are in. This is due to the investment that has been made in setting up a global support structure, the cost of translation of the software, and modifications for local laws. This will justify why international pricing is being used.

Centralized maintenance

In all circumstances, the customer must agree to one point of contact for centralized maintenance for software updates and support.

Influence

Influence is defined as the place, person or persons that can directly drive the deal and get it to signature. It will not necessarily be the person who signs the contract.

Engagement rules for multiple counties

There are various engagement rules that need to be followed.

Option 1. Local rep selling into a division in their territory but the HQ is outside of their territory

Sales reps who work on a division of a company whose headquarters are 'out of territory' must inform their manager by email that this is the case. The manager will then give authorization to engage, and also inform the HQ sales manager of the engagement. A decision will then be made by the two managers to see if they should engage the HQ at this stage as well.

NB - some divisions of multinational companies could purchase locally if priced under a certain level. If HQ is aware of this purchase they might instruct the division not to buy and a sale could be lost or delayed. Good business practice must be applied to see if the HQ needs to be contacted in this sale.

A list of large accounts that have sales reps assigned, together with their subsidiaries, will be discussed on a regular basis with sales managers and flagged in our CRM system. New fields in opportunities have been added: 'Sub of Multinational' and 'HQ of Multinational'. If the account is on this list then the HQ rep must be informed as well as the sales manager of any activity.

Option 2. Divisional rep selling into the HQ territory

This example is where a sales rep is actually selling into the territory of the HQ sales rep.

Automatic 20% drop in commission

Any deal that is out of territory will automatically have 20% of the out-of-territory deal value assigned to the HQ Rep. Once the initial deal is done, and if the HQ rep has been asked not to approach the HQ for fear of losing the account, the HQ Rep should now engage with the HQ company and continue to work with the selling rep. If the selling rep can still influence the deal outside of their territory, and is clearly driving the sale, then future sales made in the HQ territory will now attract a 50:50 split between the selling rep and the HQ rep.

NB - the selling rep, for the purposes of this deal, will act as the sales account manager for this account and the HQ rep must keep the selling rep informed at all times of any activity. The selling rep is in effect the boss of the HQ Rep for this particular deal.

The two reps will work together and failure to do this could lead to the account being taken away or the splits lost or re-assigned.

Control moves to the HQ rep

If the influence of this deal now moves to the HQ and it is clearly seen that the initial selling rep has no influence in future sales in the HQ territory - this deal will move 100% back to the HQ rep and no commission or sales credit flows back to the initial selling rep for out of territory sales for future sales.

Option 3. HQ rep selling into another rep's territory

If there is a multinational deal happening where part of the deal is dropped into another territory then if the sales rep whose territory it drops into has no influence in the deal they will still be entitled to 20% of the value of the deal in their territory, as a drop in. If it can later be shown that the sales rep has managed to up-sell additional revenue into this drop in account then future revenue will be shared 50:50.

Competitive deals

If a deal is competitive and influence is split then sales reps must get other territories involved. Why? Because it is unlikely that the competition will have a large account strategy and be willing to do demos outside of their territory. This will help to win the account.

Affiliates

Affiliates are an essential part of a sales strategy and they will uncover opportunities. If an affiliate discovers a large account opportunity then the following structure will apply:

- Affiliates will receive full credit for the deal they have found but need to hand over the deal to their country rep and HQ rep if required.
- Affiliates can't sign a deal out of territory.

Sales splits

All sales splits are based on the entire software purchase (i.e. users and modules) and the maintenance support value of the deal.

Sales Split No 1. 100 Influenced by HQ

- Contract signed at HQ, no involvement necessary by the local rep, and non competitive. 100% influence belongs to the selling rep.
- The selling rep receives 100% of the deal in their territory.
- The selling rep receives 80% of the out of territory sales value.
- The local rep receives 20% of the out of territory sales value.
- Revenue flow, based on the associated commission splits, will go to the territory for target and quota purposes as above. I.e. if the out of territory sales value is $100,000, $20,000 will be commissionable to the local rep and $20,000 of revenue will be attributed to the local rep's quota, with $80,000 being attributed to the selling rep's quota.
- New account accelerator is paid to the selling rep if it's a new account.
- No new account accelerator is paid to the local rep.
- The selling rep needs to get an estimate of the number of users and the sales value of the out-of-territory deal.
- The selling rep must ensure that there is visibility with the out-of-territory deal value to the local rep, and the local rep is responsible for ensuring that local support and training is carried out.
- The local rep gets paid at the existing install base commission rate. Future out-of-territory sales are split 50:50 if it can be shown that the local rep has a direct influence on future deals.

Sales Split No 2. Competitive Deal with Local Demos and Local Influence

- The selling rep receives 100% of the deal in their territory.
- The selling rep receives 50% of the out of territory sales value.
- The local rep receives 50% of the out of territory sales value.
- Revenue in the selling rep's territory, based on the associated commission splits, will flow to the selling rep's quota. I.e. if the out of territory sales value is $100,000, $50,000 will be commissionable to the selling rep and $50,000 of revenue will be attributed to the selling rep's quota.
- Revenue in the local rep's territory, based on the associated commission splits, will flow to the local rep's quota. I.e. $50,000 will be commissionable to the local rep and $50,000 of revenue will be attributed to the local rep's quota.
- Future out of territory sales is split 50:50.

Sales Split No 3. A deal is done in a division of a Multinational Account but, later on, it is pushed up to the HQ which is situated in another country and a contract is signed there

The deal must have been influenced from work done by the divisional selling rep in opening up the deal and the divisional selling rep can still show strong influence.

- The HQ selling rep receives commission based on 80% of the deal value in the HQ selling rep's territory.
- Divisional selling rep receives commission based on 20% of the initial new deal value.
- 20% of the initial deal value will go to the divisional selling rep's quota.
- 80% of the deal value will go to the HQ selling rep's quota.
- Once the 20% has been paid, the sales split reverts back to scenario 1 or 2 above.

All commissions for the selling rep/HQ selling rep will be at the appropriate new business accelerator rate. Commission for the local rep will be at the install base rate.

ALL OTHER SPLITS MUST BE AGREED WITH MANAGEMENT.

THIS POLICY IS FOR GUIDANCE ONLY AND MANAGEMENT RESERVES THE RIGHT TO OVERRIDE THIS AT ANY TIME.

Printed by BoD™in Norderstedt, Ge